Thomas Richard Bentley

**Considerations Upon the State of Public Affairs at the**

**Beginning of the Year 1796**

.

Thomas Richard Bentley

**Considerations Upon the State of Public Affairs at the Beginning of the Year 1796**

ISBN/EAN: 9783337724801

Printed in Europe, USA, Canada, Australia, Japan

Cover: Foto ©Suzi / pixelio.de

More available books at **www.hansebooks.com**

# CONSIDERATIONS

UPON

## THE STATE

OF .

# PUBLIC AFFAIRS

AT

## THE BEGINNING OF THE YEAR

## 1796.

———————

London:

PRINTED FOR J. OWEN, NO. 168, PICCADILLY.

———

1796.

# CONSIDERATIONS,

THE fyftem of Europe which arofe and un-folded itfelf during the fifteenth and fix-teenth centuries, remained in all its vigour during the next and the greateft part of the prefent age, till by the explofion of a new principle, and the effects of the revolution and conquefts of France, it has been violently fhaken and difturbed, and is in danger of being overwhelmed or forgotten.

It would be a vain parade of knowledge to detail from hiftory all the advantages we owe this fyftem, and a fuperfluous toil to expofe the ignorance and ingratitude of thofe who

would

would deride or abandon it.—Founded upon jealoufy and the fear of individual aggrandizement, it might fometimes impede the progrefs of improvement as well as power ; in circumfcribing the fteps of ambition, it might check the march of fcience, and retard the moral advancement of the world ; or while it provided for the general independence and fecurity by fetting limits to empires, deprive particular provinces of local advantages, and intercept the common benefits of nature. Thefe are the crimes it is charged with—have they been extenuated in my hands?

That, like all human inftitutions, this fyftem had its defects and imperfections, is a melancholy truth which I feel no inclination to deny or diffemble, but when active malice and indolent declamation have exhaufted themfelves in its impeachment, it will be difmiffed with honour and acquitted with applaufe.

An artificial barrier, and an interdicted river, though happier themes for eloquence and poetry, are not more intrinfically unjuft or injurious than commercial prohibitions, or colonial reftrictions : and during the operation and energy of its principle, this criminal fyftem had affigned

figned to all the ftates of Europe their courfe
and ftation, their relations and alliances, a juft
reftraint or a neceffary protection, while the
whole was bound together in one federal chain
fuftaining the weak and confining the powerful.
Under its falutary influence our fmall but intere-
refting quarter of the globe was gradually
moulded and combined into one vaft republic,
the independence of its feveral members afferted
and affured, the ambition of the preponderant
nations difappointed and repreffed, and finally
regarded as a treafon againft the liberty of all.

This jealoufy for more than a whole century has principally regarded the French nation, whofe immenfe population and refources,
with the extent of their territory and advantageous pofition upon the continent and the ocean,
but more than all thefe, their reftlefs character
and military talents have conftantly threatened,
during that period, the common independence
and integral fovereignties of Europe.

I have faid the French *nation*, not the king or the
government, as is the cant of artful and of fuperficial politicians; becaufe there is no error more
vulgar and illiberal than to charge upon princes
and minifters as an individual fault, the common propenfity and paffion of their country;

and

and becaufe in fact the government of France, with the abominable and abfurd fyftem of its financial adminiftration, has frequently contributed in no fmall degree to defend us from the force and fury of its numberlefs inhabitants, wafting their means and mifdirecting their efforts, which are both naturally too great and formidable for the common fecurity and repofe.

It is impoffible to caft the eye over the map, or over the hiftory of Europe, without inftantly perceiving the danger refulting from the enormous difproportion and natural preponderance of France. The fyftem of which we are fpeaking had itfelf improvidently favoured it in the beginning, for as the firft peril arofe from the power of Auftria then poffeffed of Spain, the Low Countries, and the New World, the aggrandizement of France had been defired and promoted by the other ftates, as the fole barrier and defence they could refort to, againft the ambition of that family: and from the force of prejudice and habit, they continued the fame policy, long after all this danger had fubfided, after the feparation of the empire from the hereditary dominions, and after France had become more formidable herfelf than the ftate againft which her greatnefs was to be erected.

It

It is important to call thefe circumftances to recollection, as the period of a general pacifica-tion approaches, and to confider whether it can be expedient at that time to depart in any material degree from the wifdom and policy of this fyftem, and to abandon the wholefome experience of four centuries, either from the preffure and impatience of momentary inconvenience, or for fpeculations of future and contingent advantages.

In the courfe of the following pages, I intend to confider both thefe propofitions, which have acquired more credit and created more anxiety in the world than they are entitled to. And I fhall endeavour to fhew, firft, that the ftate of this kingdom is not fuch as to compel us to any deviation from our old maxims, and policy, nor that of the enemy, if it were fo, fuch as to entitle or enable it to profit by our embarraffments. Secondly, That the ftate of the colonies or poffeffions of Europe in other quarters of the world, is not fuch as to afford any reafonable hope of our finding a counterbalance there to the predominance of France, if we were to affent to her pretenfions upon the territories fhe has conquered from our allies.

In the courfe of thefe enquiries, it will become neceffary for me to connect the war with
the

the principle of the French revolution; and that I may do so with more accuracy, I shall first treat of them separately, and afterwards combine them together, as far as they appear to me to act upon one another, and to be reciprocally causes and effects of our present dangers, apprehensions, or difficulties.

From the immense variety and importance of the objects that must pass under my consideration, I shall perhaps be forced to treat them with a degree of precision and brevity that may appear confident; I am so far, however, from feeling myself liable to any reproaches upon this account, that I can honestly affirm, that it is from anxiety for truth and correctness in positions which are intimately blended with the welfare, and perhaps the existence, of my country, that I forbear to recommend them to the imagination, and speak home to the understanding and the heart.

I have said that the balance of power was exposed by the explosion of a new principle, as well as by the effects of the war. Considering this principle in general, and without analysis or detail, it had for its object to dissolve all the existing treaties and alliances of Europe, throughout the states of which it was to render general

one

one fpecies of conftitution, and to take the whole under the protection and guaranty of France. Thus inftead of maintaining and invigorating that combination which has fo long appeared neceffary to reprefs the turbulence and ambition of that nation, we were to furrender every fortrefs and barrier into its hands, to receive its garrifons, and truft implicitly to its generofity and forbearance. It would be curious to confider the artifice and forefight with which the principal men in that country prepared from afar, and difpofed the public mind to receive fo great a fhock of opinion, and run counter to all the maxims, habits, and even prejudices of Europe. Unfortunately they received but too much countenance and affiftance from thofe who either did not perceive the danger, or were anxious to turn it to their own profit and advantage. When we look at the havoc and ruin of this part of the world, it were unwholefome to diffemble the fhare its rulers have had in it; amongft the miners and pioneers of its deftruction we may diftinguifh its princes; its mob-kings were preceded by imperial reformers, and it was torn to pieces by hands confecrated in its defence. This fyftem which had long been mocked with bitternefs and invective, was

now

now accufed as the caufe of all the wars that had
fo often defolated Europe, and which were lately
difcovered to have been wanton, unjuft, and unneceffary; and the common religion, which even
fpeaking politically, had no doubt been a principal caufe of the unrivalled profperity of this
part of the world, was expofed to the attacks
of infidel fovereigns, more fatal than the ridi-
cule of wits or philofophers.

Jofeph the Second, and Frederic the *Great*,
Staniflaus of Poland, and Lewis the Sixteenth,
were all of them reformers, and excepting the
fecond of them, they have all met with the fate
of reformers ;—it was only under their aufpices
that the Voltaires and Rouffeaus, the Mirabeaus
and Condorcets worked at the common ruin
and at their own. When pofterity fhall contem-
plate the relations of the laft fix eventful years,
its incredulity will difappear and its doubts
fubfide, becaufe it will find them preceded by
the expulfion of the monks in Flanders, by the
deftruction of the barrier in the Netherlands,
by the writings of Frederic the Second, by the
Comte Rendû and minifterial democracy of Neck-
ar—perhaps even its aftonifhment will be little
or momentary, becaufe it will have come frefh
from beholding all Europe leagued together in
defence

defence of the rebellious colonies of America, and united to pull down and annihilate the only power which could protect its liberties, and which had protected them fo often.

All thefe events and circumftances are diftinct and predifpofing caufes, of the French revolution, as they are alfo of the forced and violent pofition in which we actually find ourfelves, from the moral corruption and phyfical inequality of the world.

The *exterior* principle of this revolution, if I may be excufed that expreffion, being the deftruction of the balance of power by the diffolution of the treaties, that of Munfter or Weftphalia became their firft obftacle, and gave them the greateft embarraffment. Favourable at the time to the aggrandizement of France, it had neverthelefs defined and fixed the limits of her empire ; and befides its exprefs ftipulations had eftablifhed a principle in Europe, which with the progrefs of her ambition, and the impunity of her ufurpations, became a kind of enchanted circle, where her fpirit felt uneafy and confined. " What has France to do, fays Mirabeau, with the pretended *balance of powers?* With ten years of a good adminiftration, fhe would regain her *natural fuperiority over all Europe together?*"

c                                                        Till

Till the laft war, it was a general maxim of that cabinet, that fhe muft crufh England in the firft conteft in which that power fhould be able to create no diverfion by her alliances on the continent.—The events and circumftances of that war, produced but a very imperfect change in this fanguine perfuafion, and certainly did not materially operate upon the political opinions of France, as every perfon converfant in the writings of that country muft acknowledge. They confidered us as ruined and humiliated, and about to be deprived of our poffeffions in the Eaft Indies, as we had unfortunately been forced to abandon our colonies in the Weft. " England, fays the fame writer, whofe authority I prefer to many others upon the fame fubject, *England can do nothing.*" She is no longer the firft power, when fhe has loft the Indies (which fhe can fcarce retain for ten years) fhe will be a power of the *third* rank. He then foretells that fhe will experience commotions, and that fhe will be fprinkled with her own blood ; but in recompence for her preponderance in Europe which fhe is to forfeit, he generoufly makes her a prefent of liberty, which he declares to be incompatible with external power ; and he concludes, that France has

has nothing to apprehend from her, that fhe cannot revenge the injuries of the laft war, for fortunately, he exclaims, " *Elle n'en a pas les moyens* ; that is out of her power\*."

Not being however quite certain of de-ftroying the treaties by the nullity of Great Britain, which would effectually accomplifh that purpofe, and reftore her *natural fuperi-ority to* France *over all Europe together* ; ano-ther project was fet on foot, a kind of par-tition-treaty, by which the empire of the fea and of commerce, might be fecured to Great Britain, if, upon her part, fhe would abandon the fyftem of Europe, and affign the whole do-minion of the continent to France. And he propofes in confequence, " a folid, fincere, and eternal alliance, *founded upon a treaty of com-merce*, which fhould put an end for ever to na-tional jealoufies and bind indiffolubly the in-terefts of the two empires. " United," fays he, " they would without difficulty, impofe *filence upon the reft of the earth†*."

Thefe plans or opinions are become important and remarkable, becaufe the events of the war, in which France has made fuch enormous acquifitions upon the continent, and the arms

\* Dentes fur l'ouverture de l'Efcaut, p. 8 and 9.   † Page 21.

of Great Britain been crowned with equal fuccefs upon the ocean, have apparently given body
and confiftency to this dangerous and wicked fpeculation, and an idea has been thrown out into the
world, that the territorial ufurpations of France
might poffibly be conceded at the peace, if an
equivalent were found in the commercial and
maritime aggrandizement of Great Britain.
Though it is premature to examine this opinion, I cannot omit the firft opportunity of brand-
ing it with every epithet, due to the moft bafe
and difhonourable of all public counfels, excepting indeed, thofe, which would fubmit implicitly to the preponderance of France, without
any recompence or ftruggle, any hope of eman-
cipation or reverfion of liberty.

Another project of France, for *regaining her
natural fuperiority over all Europe together*, was
the forming the ten provinces of the Auftrian
Netherlands, into an independent republic, and
to open the navigation of the Scheldt by a war
upon the United Provinces, in which prefum-
ing the weaknefs and infignificance of England,
and the infurrections fhe would be able to excite
againft the Stadtholder, fhe had no apprehenfions of failing in fuccefs. It is to be obferved,
the Emperor, the Dutch, and Great Britain,

were

were at this time all at peace with France, yet
fhe was meditating and confpiring revolutions,
in every one of their refpective ftates.

The limits and barriers, the whole conven-
tional law of Europe, ftood in the way of
France, even the geography and diftinct appell-
ations of its provinces and people, feemed an
obftacle to her *natural fuperiority*. Frenchmen,
Dutchmen, Flemings, reminded her of treaties
which confined and coerced her, and fhe recalled
with affectation and folicitude the names of thefe
regions and people, from times preceding the civil-
ization and fettlement of this quarter of the globe,
from remote periods of antiquity, from the trea-
tife of Tacitus, and the commentaries of Cefar.
Batavians, Belgians, Allobroges, Maffilians,
every term that could fhake the habitual relations,
and exifting fyftem was difcovered and reftored: but the treaty of Munfter was expofed alfo
to a very peculiar fpecies of attack, which was
countenanced by the Emperor, who at that time
had two projects to be favoured by it, namely,
the opening of the Scheldt, and the invafion of
the liberties of Germany. Thefe were equally
guaranteed by the treaty, as the treaty itfelf
was by the principal Governments of Europe—
but it was found that this treaty being againft
the

the natural law, in as much as rivers have a
right to flow wherever they pleafe, no pofitive ftipulations
had any power to interrupt the liberty
of their courfe*. The Emperor however having
mifcalculated the ftate of public opinion, and
his own perfonal influence in the French cabinet,
was obliged finally to defift from this pretenfion
by the treaty of 1788, and that of Munfter
was refpected till it became the direct intereft
of France to infringe it.

I have adverted to this circumftance becaufe
it afterwards became the immediate caufe of the
prefent war, and is the only one that it is now,
at all neceffary *diplomatically* to affign for it, tho',
I proteft I know not why, it has been more
ufual to name others more difputable and remote, fuch as the decree of 19th Nov. 1792,
and the interference of France, in our domeftic œconomy and fituation; thefe, in my
opinion, would be more properly confidered
fimply as additional and powerful motives
for defending that treaty with greater obftinacy, becaufe they prove that at the time
the French openly attacked it, and with it
the fyftem of Europe, they endeavoured to di-
vert its guarantees from maintaining and pro-

* Annales politiques, civiles & littéraires, N . 88, 89.

tecting

tecting it, by exciting inteftine difturbances
and commotions in their refpective ftates. It is
in purfuance of the plan I have laid down, that
I am thus careful to feparate the principle of the
French revolution from the caufe of the war,
though I have no fcruple to affert that nothing
but the war could have turned the courfe and
eluded the violence of the revolution :—that
it brought the loaded cloud nearer to us I will
not deny, but it has guided the bolt over our
heads, and difcharged it into the earth, harm-
lefs and fpent forever.

Having difembarraffed the caufe of hoftilities
from all thofe collateral circumftances with
which it is connected, and reduced it to the
fimple violation of the treaty of Weftphalia, in
the pretenfions and invafion of the French upon
Holland, in the beginning of the year 1793, I
fhall confider the contagion and danger of their
principles and their machinations in the bofom
of foreign ftates, under a totally diftinct head,
when I come to examine the remaining obfta-
cles to peace and negociation.

The French being thus clearly aggreffors in
the war, it remains defenfive on the part of
Great Britain and her allies, unlefs, which I do
not recollect, they have ever offered reftitution
and

and indemnity for the injury. If they ever
have done fo, I am willing to confefs that it has
changed its nature, and become unjuft and ambitious upon our part ; but till this fact is pointed
out and afcertained to me, I can difcover only
the injuftice and ambition of thofe, who belie,
if they do not betray, the caufe of their country.

Wars, fay the civilians, are not maffacres and
confufions, but the higheft trials of right, when
princes and ftates put themfelves upon the juftice of God for the deciding of their controver-
fies, by fuch fuccefs as it fhall pleafe him to
award on either fide. The war therefore may
be confidered as an appeal to Heaven, and
though to prove it defenfive on our part, we
need affign to men no other proofs than the
violation of the treaty and actual invafion on the
part of France, yet in fubmitting our caufe
to the great Judge and Difpofer of Events, we
have the confolation to know that it is defenfive, not of the Scheldt only, or of the fields of
Flanders, but of our liberty, our conftitution,
and our religion, but of his laws and our own.

If we are to feek his judgment however in
the actual circumftances of the war, it is impoffible to conceal that we have experienced
many calamities and difafters, fome indeed that
are

are infeparable from war, others arifing from
our own miftakes and errors, and ftill others
more dreadful than all, from the vifitation of
difeafe and the fury of the elements. It is no
difcovery of to-day, nor of the philofophy of
to-day, that *war* is an evil, nor that it is followed by a train of evils, nor that it has been
frequently provoked by the violence of a
king or the paffions of a people ; but it would be
extraordinary indeed, if a fpirit which neither
piety nor reafon, neither faith nor philofophy
have been able to fubdue, fhould vanifh at the
bidding of his fellow-devil Sedition. I confefs
my aftonifhment is not excited only, but my
indignation alfo, at all that cant and whining
which have overwhelmed the prefs, and the de-
bates of both houfes of Parliament, and at
thofe perfidious tears which fall *fix times
a week* over the unavoidable calamities that
purfue its fteps, becaufe I obferve them to pro-
ceed from men, more anxious to call it nearer
home, and to light it up in the bofom of their
country, than to drive it to the confines of the
earth, or extinguifh it altogether.

Thofe who would run the rifk of *civil* war,
cannot take it ill if I fufpect them of exagge-
rating in fome degree the antipathy they bear

D                                    to

to *foreign* war. Thofe who extract the immorality from infurrection and revolt, who reduce fedition and rebellion, fo long taught as a fcience and a duty, to a frigid calculation of prudence, and apprehend nothing from violence and treafon, but the improbability of their fuccefs.—— Thofe who would turn our fwords into *our own* bofoms, and fhed our blood in *our own* fields, have no reafon to be offended if it is not only to the delicacy of their nerves, and the excefs of their fenfibility that I attribute a part of the repugnance they exprefs at the fpectacle of our contefts with *rival* and *hoftile nations.*

War, however, is an evil, and no men can be more fenfible that it is fo, than they whofe duty it is to declare its neceffity, and announce the fatal fentence to their country—They act under a dreadful refponfibility to the laws, to public opinion, to pofterity, and to heaven. It is not the whining of the prefs, it is not the phrafe-factory of the oppofition, that can deplore or exprefs the evils of war, as they are felt by thofe, who every moment compare them with the evils which are avoided by war; who make the eftimate and fet-off in their bofoms, and weigh the blood which flows, with the

caufe

caufe that demands it—But when all its miferies are numbered and detailed, there is a balance to be ftruck at home, and a comparifon to
be adjufted abroad. On the one fide, we fee our
fields remain with their ancient proprietors, the
laws maintained, and juftice adminiftered, our
temples unpolluted, and our conftitution perfect on its bafe. On the other, when we con-
template the ftate of our enemies, we do not
find them exempted from impartial calamity,
the war has dealt out deftruction with an equal
hand, and meafured the difafters of mankind.

> Sunt illis fua funera, parque per omnes
> Tempeftas.

I fee the ocean covered with their defeats,
and the forefts of Germany reeking with
their blood : and turning from that difgufting
fpectacle to their interior fituation, what do I
behold in the wide defart of their empire, but
a pale and emaciated people, expiring with famine, or fainting with fatigue and oppreffion ?
I fee their fufferings and their groans ftrike upon
my ears, but I cannot difcover the religion, or
the juftice, or the fundamental laws for which
they are fighting ; I do not find the hufband-

man

man in the fields, nor the merchant in his counting-houfe, nor the cities upon their foundations, nor in the caufe for which they are contending any thing that is refpectable but the enchanting name of their country!

Yet for this I find them brave every thing, and bear every thing, and am compelled to admire their miftaken patriotifm, as well as their military prowefs, and their political refolution.

Imagination cannot paint a fpecies or excefs of mifery, which they have not felt and complained of; they have endured and perpetrated every horror, and fuffered the action and re-action of every crime, with a name or without one; full of indignation and remorfe, afhamed of the paft, and hopelefs of the future, they derive a conftancy from defpair, and perfevere in the inextinguifhable defire of *aggrandizing* their country—their country, which panting at the heart, and bleeding at every pore, affumes the attitude and language of a conqueror, and dictates the terms of an infulting peace, with a firm voice and an impofing countenance.

It would be ungenerous to with-hold applaufe from a fpectacle like this; there has been a time when it would have been the admiration of Britifh patriots, when it would have
been

been the language of thofe who afpired to popularity, to bid us alfo, to dare and fuffer all for
our country; and when this part of the conduct
of France would have been felected for the example of Englifhmen, rather than that fpirit of
infubordination and anarchy which are the true
caufes of all the mifery and diftrefs of our unhappy enemies.  Is it not furprizing that thofe
who take fo deep an intereft in all the reft of
their fituation, fhould fee nothing great or ge-
nerous in devoting themfelves for their country?
and for what a country? while, on the contrary, they have preached to their own a bafe
and cowardly defpondency, an abject and almoft
unqualified fubmiffion, under the firft fcratches
of the war? but what do they difcover in the
character of Englifhmen fo new and degenerate,
as to make them expect, that we will quit the
gay and gallant veffel which we navigate, or
ftrike our flag to a wreck—to a wreck which
our arms have made, and the ftorm toffes without a rudder or a pilot, in which all that is interefting is the defpair and affection of the
wretches that cling to her?

It is unneceffary for me to make the comparifon in detail between the actual pofition of the
contending countries.  The internal ftate of
France

France has lately been demonſtrated to the
world with much accuracy and preciſion, in an
excellent treatiſe upon their revolution and
finances, which has been read and admired by
every perſon of judgment and good informa-
tion. I have conſequently not many remarks,
to ſet down upon that important ſubjeƈt ; and no
very material details excepting upon circumſtances which have ariſen ſubſequent to that publi-
cation ; and upon the other ſide, I ſhall confine
myſelf in the ſame manner to the notice of a
few of the leading and prominent features in our
own ſituation and circumſtances.

With reſpeƈt to the depreciation of the aſſig-
nats, which at the time I write is liv. 5000=24 gold
or preciſely 201=1 I confeſs my ſcepticiſm as to
all reaſoning and calculation that can be formed
upon it ; notwithſtanding the decay and languor it experiences, there is a principle
about it, which would make me unhappy,
if I foreſaw no proſpeƈt of pacification till it ex-
pired, I ſhould be ſorry indeed that we had nothing but a reverſion in the peace, and that the
war was at any rate to terminate only with the
funeral of this paper.

In my opinion, the actual reſources of a
country are nothing elſe than its phyſical reſources,

fources, namely, its population, fubfiftences, and capital, together with the faculty of re-production it poffeffes in the induftry of its fields and towns; I confider the credit of a ftate as very diftinct from its property; that it arifes from the opinion or experience of its good faith and folvency, that it is limited and proportioned to its real poffeffions, and is fo far from adding any thing *pofitive* to its refources, that it diminifhes them at any given period of time, by having acted before as an artificial capital, and confequently enabled it to difpenfe with a part of the real, which muft otherwife have remained at home, if it were merely as the machine and vehicle of its commerce.

I have faid *at any given time*, becaufe no man can be more fenfible than myfelf, of the *growing* and *progreffive* advantages derived from it, and from the very circumftances I have mentioned. But thefe confiderations are foreign to the immediate fubject of difcuffion. It feems certain that in the moft profperous times the credit of a country can never be pufhed beyond its fuppofed faculties of repayment, and in periods of exigency, that, if it could be fo, it would be fo far from being entitled to be confidered as an advantage or a refource, that it would

would add the greateft weight to its decline and ruin.

A great part of the phyfical refources of a country are at the difpofal of regular governments, and are conftantly contributed, though the operation is indirect, complex, and frequently imperceptible. The credit of the ftate is the moft circuitous way of arriving at them, and confequently the worft ; for it is nothing elfe but a previous mortgage of the national property for the intereft and reduction of debts which are afterwards to be provided for by a more direct contribution ; and the public thus pays not only what is right and neceffary to the exigencies of the Government, but an additional premium to the lender. It does not only pay the whole amount of the taxes, with the expences of levying them, but an indemnity or recompence to the individuals who have advanced them in the firft inftance to the ftate.

As a *refource* therefore, we find, in fact, that in well regulated ftates, their credit is never applied to but in moments of exigency, arifing out of wars, which the prefent ftate of fociety in this quarter of the world, permits to be waged with more fury and violence, but happily during fhorter periods of time, than is the

cafe

cafe with lefs civilized nations. Between thefe
we may obferve wars progreffively feeble, but
longer and more implacable, and as they recede
farther from the arts and improvements of fociety, languid and eternal.

I confider credit therefore as a fudden and
ruinous way of arriving at the contributions,
rendered indeed indifpenfible by the nature of
the modern wars of Europe, but not to be
counted abftractedly as one of the refources of a
country.

I am inclined, in the fame manner, to look
upon the affignat implicitly, as an indirect me-
thod adopted by the Government in France, of
laying their hands upon the real refources of
that country* : which mode of confidering it, if
I am not miftaken, will lead to more certain
conclufions, than the complex and metaphyfical manner of treating it as the fole fund poffeffed by them for the carrying on of the war.

Before it had declined through half the fpace
of its prefent depreciation, I confefs it ap-

* " La Politique," fays Efchafferiaux, in the name of the
commiffion of five, upon the caufes of the fituation of the
finances, 22 Brumaire, (Oct. 13.) " Régarde les affignats
comme un inftrument, que la révolution a ufé entre les mains
de la nation ; la diminution de leur valeur comme un *impôt*
infenfible, qui a péfé fur tous les citoyens."

peared

peared to me probable that it would have ope-
rated fome very important change in the adminiftration of the finances, and reduced the Government to the neceffity of ufing very extraordinary and eccentric means for arriving at the
refources for which it had occafion ; and though
my expectations have not been realized fo early
as I imagined, I think that the period cannot
be much longer delayed, and even that I perceive the beginning of it.

Always looking upon the affignats in the
light I have mentioned, I own I never expected that even their complete annihilation (though
hope and neceffity will perhaps cling to them
much longer than can be conceived or explained) would induce an indifpenfable neceffity for
peace. There appeared to me another *integral
period* of difficulty and diftrefs, through which
the pride and pertinacity of France might ftill
ftruggle, before fhe arrived at the boundaries
of diforganization, and emerged into the Tar-
tar barbarifm which feems the object and crown
of her inverted fyftem.

The precious metals have long difappeared
and been difpenfed with; after full four years
of decreafe and decline, they have become extinct.
or invifible in the internal commerce and tranf-
actions

actions of the country;* though they have from
time to time re-produced themfelves in the *actual* plunder of the government, or the fpeculations of the ftock-jobbers in the rue Vivienne
and the Palais-Egalité.—Having fupplied their
place by a currency, to which enthufiafm
at firft, and afterwards neceffity and terror
gave the impulfe it required, it is no wonder
that the government fhould have been aftonifhed
at the unexpected means it found in its power,
not only by the credit given to its paper, but
from fo great a part of the fpecie of the empire,
which being replaced by a new fign, they were
enabled to tranfport into the neutral countries,
which fupplied them with the fuel and materials of war.

But as this enthufiafm fubfided by degrees,
and the fyftem of terror received at leaft a violent interruption and difcredit, I obferved the
depreciation to tumble with accelerated velocity, and from the enormity of the fums iffued
by the treafury, I expected that it would conti-

---

* We cannot calculate that there exifts in circulation more
than two or three hundred millions in fpecie, (= to 8 or 12
millions fterling) and even thefe are in the departments upon
the frontiers, &c. *Le Brun, report to the council of elders in
the name of the commiffion of finance, Dec. 3d.* 1795.

nue

nue to deſcend with progreſſive rapidity. There remained, however, another experiment, which would preſent ſociety under a new face, and which I thought it likely that extraordinary people would endeavour to realize ; namely, to diſpenſe with any ſign altogether, and reduce every contract and tranſaction to the ſimple and original operation of barter, or the exchange of one commodity for another, and a direct contribution of the public impoſitions in kind.

If I am not miſtaken, they are now adopting this deſign, (of which they might have derived the idea from ſome of the colonies of Engliſh America) and that it is their intention to diſpenſe with all intermediate ſigns of value, and make the compariſon direct with the weight or meaſure of corn. I obſerve that all the ſalaries of the officers of ſtate, &c. under the new conſtitution, are fixed at ſo many quintals of wheat. The contribution called the *forced loan*, is payable in grain, and magazines are to be erected by the government, for their reception ; and there is room to believe, that the ſtamp duties and others, which by the late regulations are demanded in ſpecie, will be, or are all convertible into payments in grain ; ſo that I think it

poſſible

poffible, that this ftaple will quickly become the fole ftandard of values in the empire.

It is proper that I fhould remark here, that by the Tarif fettled by the legiflature at the end of the laft year (1795) for the currency of the affignats, it is impoffible that either grain or fpecie fhould enter voluntarily into the granaries or coffers of the republic, becaufe the value being fixed at one hundred livres for one of the nominal value of the affignat, and the affignat being as I have mentioned above, at a difcount upon change of more than twice that fum, every contributor will fave a full half of his contingent, by making his payment in that paper. If the *forced loan*, therefore, and the other impofitions are really exacted, the government will commence by withdrawing the affignats from circulation, and finifh by receiving the taxes in kind; for by the confeffion of the minifter of finance*, I am authorized to affert, what

---

* Report of Faipoul to the Executive Directory, Dec. 12.

" In four lines," fays this minifter, " the following is the ftate of the public treafury.

" It owes feventy-two millions in *fpecie*, twenty millions in bills upon Spain require time—one hundred millions of affignats per day, have not hitherto fupplied a third part of the fum wanted.

what I would otherwife very willingly have taken upon my own refponfibility, that the whole fpecie in the empire, is inadequate to replace that fign of values.

By the total difappearance of an intermediate fign, if I do not deceive myfelf, the government hopes to be able virtually to renew the *maximum*, and lay hands *directly* upon the articles of neceffity ; and fuppofing the endurance and apathy of the people, it is not improbable that they may fucceed in it for a moment. When the contributions are taken in kind, they will be no longer levied in the counting houfe, but from the ftacks and granaries of the farmers, the fhoemaker will be taxed to furnifh a certain number of fhoes, the clothier will be called upon in his turn, the government will erect magazines and ftore-houfes in every diftrict, and the fyftem of public contributions be a direct and general requifition*.

This

wanted. Fifteen hundred millions which will be paid within this decade, will produce but a feeble fenfation.

" Citizens Directors, fuch is the afflicting portrait, &c. We muft have meafures to put an end to this frightful fituation of affairs."

* There is one object which effentially demands your folicitude ; it is the execution of the law which orders the payment

This is the crifis into which I imagine the
French government will be thrown by the continued depreciation or extinction of the affignats,
and not into the direct and immediate neceffity
of defifting from hoftilities, as is prefumed by
the gentleman to whom I have alluded, and
feems to be very generally adopted as an article
of political faith in this couutry. It will not
appear, however, that the difference of opinion
is fatal between us, becaufe I confider this crifis
as being of neceffarily very fhort duration, and
that it will quickly conduct them to the period
expected by him. But as I have obferved from
the delay and procraftination that attends the
realizing of any opinion, men are not only dif-
pirited and difappointed, but led to defpair, and
to conclude, frequently to direct contraries, as
people confined by bad weather, cry out at laft
that it will *never* be fine, I have wifhed to in-
dicate the fole obftacle I think likely to happen,
if France fhould adhere to that principle of con-

ment *in kind* of one half of the contribution, for the third year
of the republic, (1795).

*Letter of the minifter of the interior, 22d. Brumaire.*

In the fame letter he demands from the adminiftrators of
the departments, an account of the *cattle, corn, wine, fruits,
hemp, &c.*

if

queft, which will make fuch an event abfolutely
neceffary to the peace, independence, and tranquillity of Europe.

I do not think it neceffary to take much
notice in detail of the cedule and the new
projeft of finance, though it might expofe me
to mifreprefentation if I were to omit it altogether: it appears to me then, both vifionary
and wicked; to fet up a counter-paper to the
affignat, and to coin fpecie, is to attempt what
is abfurd and what is impoffible. But I am inclined to confider it as a meafure invented by the
Government, to facilitate the defign I have fug-
gefted, and withdraw the figns of value altogether; becaufe the very aft of decreeing a better
fecurity, than that of the mortgage of the affignats, is the moft violent and indecent mock-
ery of the public faith, and muft effectually extinguifh all confidence in any paper whatever,
and the creating a quantity of metals equal to
reprefent and fupply it, is, I imagine, an abfolute and real impoffibility.

Of their late reverfes upon the Rhine, the
feries of defeats they have fuffered, and the entire lofs of their army in the Palatinate, I do
not think it fo neceffary to enquire into the
probable effects, as into the immediate caufes,

becaufe

becaufe I fhould think it very fuperficial
and weak to affign them exclufively to the fkill
and bravery of the Imperial generals and armies,
or to any particular defect or even inferiority in
thefe refpects, of the forces and commanders
of the Republic.—Certainly it would at leaft
be illiberal to conclude that they had not con-
ducted themfelves upon thefe trying occafions,
with all the valour and addrefs, which have
long rendered them fo formidable in the eyes of
Europe. But it is not of fo much importance to
remark thefe wounds, which however deep
might not be incurable, or thefe calamities,
which however dreadful might not yet be irreparable ; as the caufes of them, which feem to
affure that they are incurable and irreparable indeed. When we learn* that the army captured in
Manheim was deficient in *two-thirds* of its number, by defertion and the total ftoppage of re-
cruiting ; when we attend to the complaints of
the Generals, the fubfequent meafures of the
directors for the fupply of the armies of the
north, and the increafed feverity of the laws
againft deferters, at the end of November, can
we hefitate to pronounce the progrefs of depopu-

* Vide Gazette Extraordinary, Dec. 11th, 1795.

F                                            tion

lation and famine, or doubt the real exhaufture and emptinefs of the empire ?

The moral and political ftate of this unfortunate country, is the next point of view in which I think it important to confider her. Hitherto I have endeavoured to point out the bafis and conditions of a juft and adequate pacification, by unavoidable conceffions upon her part, but the prefent difcuffion involves the wifdom and propriety, nay, the poffibility of making peace with her at all. For unlefs thofe who are her advocates, or think themfelves her advocates, were egregioufly miftaken in fome of their affertions, it would be out of the power of this country, with all its fuperiority and advantages, to come to a negotiation. It is confoling in this refpect to obferve, that by the experience which the world has feen, and France herfelf has acknowledged, of the evils arifing from her extravagant doctrines and principles, by the fucceffive downfall and difcredit of all her provifional conftitutions, by the difgrace and difperfion of her clubs and correfponding focieties, and by the infamous death and punifhment of fo many of her fanatical leaders, by her return towards moderation, by the abjuration of her tenets, and the purging of her Pantheon, the conteft is become lefs

complicated

complicated and difficult, and the war reduced
upon her fide to a fimple war of ambition and
aggrandizement, in which I have already endeavoured to afcertain her pretenfions and title
to fuccefs.

There is no longer any queftion with what
form of government, or defcription of perfons,
it is eligible to negociate. If ever there was any
thing of opinion in the caufes of this war, it
has long fince fubfided and been at reft. France
herfelf has extinguifhed it in torrents of her
blood, and fealed it with her own interdiction
and anathema. But I know there are perfons
who teach, if they do not believe, that her
principles are triumphant becaufe her *republic
will be acknowledged* at a general pacification ;
fuch a doctrine would be contemptible as well
as abfurd, if it were not propagated with the
moft malicious and dangerous defign, namely,
to nourifh and inflame thofe principles where
indeed they have triumphed, if it be triumph
to miflead and corrupt the ignorant and un-
wary, to join with the weak and the wicked,
the reprobates and outcafts of every fociety, to
ally and confederate with vice and folly, and
finally with mifery and impatience, with the ine-
vitable hardfhips and repinings of the human

race

race and condition. Here indeed they have been welcomed, but even here they are obliged to diffemble and conceal themfelves, to hide their fhame, and to mafk their deformity.

But it is not in the eftablifhment of a republic that the revolutionary principle would have triumphed, if it had not been crufhed and ftrangled by that very republic in its cradle. It was in the *republic* of *Great-Britain*, in the *republic* of *Spain*, and of the *Empire*, in that of the *whole world*, that it was to rear the ftandard of victory; and what a republic? Not fuch as France has now founded for herfelf, compofed of orders, ftates, degrees, and gradations, (no matter with what fymmetry or coherence); not a republic of kings, and patricians, and commons, as it has now inftituted (I do not enquire with what temperament and proportion) but a republic of anarchy and confufion, of confifcation and pillage, of divorces and murder ; a republic of *fans culottes*, that is to fay, of proftitutes and ruffians, of ravifhers and robbers ; a republic of theft and force, of brutal violence and luft, a community of property and of women !

If we are to feek for the principles of the revolution, they are fo far from having triumphed in France, that they are difavowed and exe-

crated

crated by all parties and defcriptions in that country ; they are to be found however, and to be found in their ftatute book, but not in triumph, not even in exiftence, but cancelled and repealed, branded with infamy, and devoted with the tears and curfes of twenty millions of human beings.

But they are to be found in our diforganizing clubs and focieties, whither they feem to have fled before the firft fteps of returning wifdom and morality in France ; they are to be found amongft the affaffins of kings and the fubverters of conftitutions, in the caverns of guilt, fpeculation, and defpair.

The firft principle of the revolution was to break the leagues and confederacies of Europe, and the mode of action was not only the dethronement but the murder of kings. Where is the regiment of fourteen hundred affaffins, called Tyrannicides, in the new vocabulary of *ufeful* crimes and *juftifiable* murders, that were decreed in the convention ? Let us read the comments that are circulated in France, upon the outrage of the Englifh Jacobins againft his Majefty's perfon in his paffage to parliament ; it is impoffible to fpeak of that crime in any terms of horror and execration, in which it is not reprobated

ed by the journalifts of France. The Courier
Français and the Courier Univerfel in particular,
reprove one of the deputies of the convention,
for the manner in which he had fpoken of it,
" as if, they fay, any nation would treat with a
people that rejoices in the crimes and miferies
of every other." Another paper, under the
head of " revolutionary movements at London,"
enters more minutely into the fubject, and la-
ments with a deepnefs and fincerity of forrow
that might well become every Englifhman to feel
and exprefs, the poffibility of any revolution
being attempted in England. Has the principle, therefore, of *tyrannicide* triumphed ?
does it furvive any where but in the den of
Englifh anarchifts and confounders, and is it
not criminated even by their quondam confede-
rates in France ?

Has the principle of *equality* proved triumphant ? let us look at the robes of ftate, the
pretorian guards, and the enormous falaries of
the *five lords of the monarchy in commiffion*; let
us look too at the council of ancients, (their up-
per houfe of parliament) at their habits of cere-
mony, their falaries too, their guards, and the
royal palaces they both inhabit. Has not equality been defined and frittered away to mean
nothing

nothing but equality before the law, a right to
be tried by the fame tribunals, or to be candidate
for the fame employments? an equality more
fully enjoyed in England for more than a century at leaft, than it can be poffible for France,
fuppofing an immediate end to her commotions,
to enjoy it for a century to come. By the third
article of the declaration of rights, which is to
be confidered as a kind of preamble to the conftitution, *hereditary* rank is indeed formally abo-
lifhed, that is, as far as it is capable of being fo
by a declaration : but hereditary honours, and
the importance attached to birth and particular
families, cannot be deftroyed by any pofitive law
or inftitution, or hindered from giving favour
and authority to the pretenfions of candidates,
fo that the defcendants of great and popular
perfons, will continue to have an advantage
over new and unknown ones, and the part of
this principle which appears to be adopted, is
trivial or nugatory fo far as it regards *the people.* But is any equality of property or condition, which is *their* promifed equality, triumphant? The very *firft* article of the declaration of rights, takes property under its protection, and it is farther fecured by the 358*th* provifion of the conftitution ; fo that equality has
fhared

fhared the fate of tyrannicide, that is to fay, after having fpent its rage and covered France with crimes and calamities, it has been confined to fhame and forgetfulnefs. But it is important to keep its infamy alive, and in memory, as a negative example to France herfelf, to Europe, and to pofterity.

Has the principle of *annual legiflatures* and *univerfal fuffrage* proved triumphant? The legiflative affemblies are renewed partially every year, namely in one third part, which is exactly equivalent to a triennial re-election of the whole\*; But the right of voting is fo far from being univerfal, that it is limited to property, and to the contribution of property, for though it is declared † that every *citizen* has an equal right to vote for the reprefentatives, &c. the right of *citizenfhip* is afterwards reftricted † to thofe who pay a direct contribution, real or perfonal, to refidents, and to perfons infcribed in the regifter of the diftrict, and every fpecies of domeftic fervant is exprefsly deprived of it during his continuance in that fituation‡; fo that neither of thefe prin-

* Art. 53, de la conftitution.
† 8th Article of the Declaration of Rights.
† In the 8th article of the conftitution.
‡ Title 2d of the conftitution. Art. 10, and fubfequent Art.

ciples,

ciples, I imagine, will be pronounced to have been triumphant.

I now come to fpeak of another principle, the triumph of which under our own peculiar cir-cumftances at this time, might have been of no trifling importance ; but fortunately, the expe-rience and confequently the defeat of it, in France, have preceded the firft, and facilitated the other in this country ; namely, the princi-ple of *clubs, affociations, public harangues, de-bates and correfpondences.* I had originally in-, tended to have extracted fome part of the fpeeches of Bourdon, Tallien, Legendre, and others of the principal orators in France, from the denunciations which took place previous to the fhutting up of the Jacobins, and from the reports which preceded the abolition of the po-pular focieties*. But I abftain from them ; for I will not found any thing upon the confeffions or fentiments of men, without much probity or fhame. I do not confider their opinions upon moft topics to be totally exempt from intereft-ednefs, *occafionality*, and violence ; and the fup-preffion of the clubs being now made a part of the *fundamental* and *unalterable* laws of the Re-public ; I fhall be able to eftablifh this part of

* Sixth fructidor, Auguft, 22. 1793.

my

my argument with more certainty, precifion, and force, from the provifions of the conftitution itfelf.

By that conftitution it is ordained,

That " there cannot be formed any corporations or affociations contrary to the public order *."

That " no affembly of citizens fhall take the name of popular fociety†."

That " no particular fociety occupying itfelf in (the difcuffion of) political fubjects, can *correfpond* with any other, nor *affiliate* itfelf with it, nor hold *public* fittings, compofed of the members and affiftants (or auditors), diftinguifhed from each other, nor impofe conditions of *election* or *admiffion*, nor affume the right of *excluding*, nor caufe its members to carry any outward fign of their affociation‡."

" That the citizens cannot exercife their political rights out of the primary affemblies, or thofe of the communes.||"

That the citizens are at liberty to addrefs petitions to the public authorities ; but they muft be *individual* petitions. *No affociation* can pre-

* Conftitution, Art. 1. Tit. 14.
† Art. 360.
‡ Conft. Art. 362.  § Conft. Art. 363.

be

fent them in their collective capacity, excepting
the conftituted authorities; and thefe only upon
account of objects peculiar to their own departments" (or attribution).

"The petitioners muft not forget the *refpect*
due to the conftituted authorities\*."

And by that conftitution it is ordained, "that
every groupe, mob, or affemblage (attroupe-
ment) of the people is to be *inftantly difperfed* at
the *word of command,* or to be attacked by the
*military.*"

This is the actual ftate of liberty in France as
it regards popular meetings, affemblages of the
people in the ftreets or fields, clubs, lectures,
debates, even the facred and inalienable right of
petition; and I imagine that not even thofe perfons who *fuffer* moft under the action of the late
bills for the fecurity of his Majefty's perfon,
and the coercion of feditious meetings, not even
Mr. *Thelwall* himfelf, will be willing to exchange our exifting laws upon thefe objects for
thofe of our neighbouring republic, where it is
not eafy to perceive how any man can get a direct livelihood by preaching againft the government and conftitution.

It is remarkable, however, and it leads me to

\* Conft. Art. 364,

the

the collateral confideration of another revolutionary principle of no mean importance, which
had well nigh efcaped me in the croud, namely,
that of the *fovereignty* of the majority of individuals of every fociety ; I fay, it is remarkable
that upon this occafion none of the demagogues
have thought proper to remind the green and
unfledged republicans of France of their *right to
refift* and of *prudent infurrections* the moft
facred of all their duties. It is, indeed, altogether extraordinary, and fhews the effect of a
dreadful experience both upon the popular
leaders and upon the people. The firft, no doubt,
are become afraid of the violent machine
they can fet in motion, but can never controul ;
and the fecond, weary of being difturbed to no
end, and agitated without direction or object,
defire nothing but an indolent repofe, and will
yield their metaphyfical fceptre to any hand,
not only that can govern them well, but that
can govern them at all.

With the fovereignty of the people atheifm
feems to have fallen to the ground. Atheifm
fo convenient to the doctrine of facred, or of
prudent revolt. "The people\* purfued by fo

* Vide a Parifian Journalift, extracted in the 29th number
of M. Peltier's Paris, p. 241.

many

many calamities, demand only a change in their
condition——they fhew upon every occafion *the
greateft averfion to political affairs*—in the country and the cities the churches are every where
crowded with a pious people, pouring out their
regrets in the bofom of *religion.*" —With
the fovereignty and the philofophy of the people another principle of the revolution has been
extinguifhed, namely that of public proftitution,
of the arbitrary divorce of wives by hufbands
and of hufbands by wives*. The political ftate of
women, their rights and liberties have difappeared out of the new code of the conftitution;
but to purity, to domeftic happinefs and. honour, the fource of every private and public
good, to the nice relations of tendernefs and
fentiment there is no return; the delicate fex
that even " the airs of heaven may vifit too
rudely," withers and fades with the firft breath
of vice, the morals of the people, according to
their own mutual accufations and confeffions,
are entirely vitiated—vitiated I fear irretrievably ;
for of all the barriers and Alps that lay between
France and liberty, the moft impenetrable, the
moft infurmountable, the moft impervious is the

* The laws refpecting divorces were fufpended by a decree
of the Convention, Aug. 2, 1795—(15 thermidor.)

extreme and univerfal corruption of their manners, a corruption which, as far as I have had
any opportunity of obferving, is at once that of
brutal luxury and barbarous refinement.

The principles of the revolutionary fyftem
having been therefore completely unfolded,
are very generally exploded in France, and
their whole force of poifon may be regarded
as fpent and evaporated; a circumftance I beg
leave to infift upon the more, becaufe I am
ready to confefs, that if I did not regard it as
having effectually taken place, I would never
advife nor confent to a pacification with that
country, in any cafe fhort of an abfolute neceffity, arifing out of our own calamities and exhaufture, out of an *actual* weaknefs and inability.
But fortunately, not only thofe principles have
perifhed, but the authors and heroes of them,
whofe fate has been juftly implicated with the
pernicious and deftructive doctrines upon which
they built their fugitive popularity and greatnefs; I fay *fortunately*, not that I rejoice in the
fufferings and punifhment of thofe unhappy
perfons, for to me wickednefs itfelf is pitiable in
its retribution; it is in triumph and fuccefs
alone, that it is an object of vengeance or hatred;
but becaufe fuch examples are neceffary to imprefs,

prefs the obtufe capacity of the multitude, to deter and terrify, for ages to come, and to mark, by vifible examples, the expiation of public guilt, and the periods of returning juftice and reafon.

It is not the men whofe perfonal flagitiouf- nefs and crimes; it is not they whofe atrocity and ferocioufnefs, whofe invention and refinement, whofe excefs and obduracy in guilt, have difho- noured, not France alone, but human nature, that I fhould felect from the common and undif- tinguifhing atonement. It is not the Heberts and Chaumettes, the Marats and Dantons, the Carriers and Robefpierres; but the perfons who made pretence to virtue and philofophy, and abftained themfelves from the general immora- lity, they let loofe upon their country, that I fhould hold up to mark the downfal of the fa- naticifm they preached. Petion and Roland, Briffot and Condorcet, the meteor heroes of the revolution, where are they, and their coadjutors and difciples? If one of them has efcaped the common fate of his companions, or if they could cry from the tomb, they would fpeak, I think in the words of the poet:

Infanda per orbem
Supplicia et fcelerum pœnas expendimus omnes!

Since

Since I am upon the subject of these unfortunate persons, it occurs to me to say a few words
upon their peculiar enthusiam, and to consi-
der the principles of the revolution in what
may be called their *beau jour*, their best
point of view, to throw a glance over that
amiable and seductive side which they first
presented to sensible and sanguine goodness,
just as they offered afterwards equality and li-
centiousness to the sensual and corrupted. This
may be called the philosophy *par excellence* of
the revolution, and deserves a much longer and
more careful consideration than falls within the
scope and utility of my present design. It is indeed so mixed and blended with whatever can
ravish or enchant the imagination, whatever is
pleasing to admit in idea or abstraction ; so amiable in error, so delightful in extravagance, that
it is painful to the strongest minds to return
from it towards the dullness of truth and reality.
It is no wonder, therefore, that so many ardent
and susceptible spirits should prefer to remain in
an enchanted labyrinth of their own creation,
without track or limits, to travelling in the
rough and hackneyed path of practicable virtue
and attainable perfection.

This is the natural error of all those who
speculate

fpeculate upon public good, in fituations which preclude them from any great probability of contributing to it, by any thing elfe but their fpeculations; as they never expect to be called into action, or that the promifes they give will one day be demanded at their hands, they grant with a boundlefs generofity, and blefs with a perpetual giving hand. And furely, it would be cruel and illiberal to withhold any thing of what is fo eafy to part with as metaphyfical benevolence and wifdom, of what is fo well received abroad, and is fo unprofitable or pernicious at home.

The misfortune of France, in the outfet of her revolution (a misfortune from which all the reft have derived in a right and lineal fuccef-fion) was, that her philofophers who made it, were never educated nor intended to have power, nor could ever dream themfelves of pof-feffing it ; hence they fcattered abftract and vi-fionary notions with an incautious hand, impru-dent and irrefponfible, creating Eutopias and Oceanas, Societies and Commonwealths, of which the firft and moft glaring abfurdity is, that they never could be inhabited by human beings, by citizens of flefh and blood.

While they groaned over the vices and pal-

H                                            pable

pable corruptions of governments, they forgot
the imperfections of nature and the frailty of
man ; and paffing a general act of amnefty and
oblivion for the common faults and weakneffes
of humanity, they were careful to except thofe
perfons upon whom were caft the great parts
and characters in the drama of the world. Upon
them they charged the crimes, the miferies,
and the ignorance of the great body of our race,
whom nature has condemned by an indifpenfible condition of exiftence, to cultivate or conquer
her in the fields, and to fupply or imitate her in
the cities. Unfortunately their own government was too guilty of a great part of the accu-
fation, to be able to repel the reft ; for the la-
bouring claffes were oppreffed and degraded by
a pernicious fyftem of finance, and feodality
to a degree that made it hard to feparate
and diftinguifh the natural from the political
evil.

I haften over this interefting and important
fubject, which I wifh rather to point out than
inveftigate, and confine myfelf to obferve, that
if the philofophy that undertook to relieve thefe
grievances, had been able to analyze and attribute them to their true caufes, it might have removed the political ill, without corrupting the

moral

moral agent, or difturbing the natural condition ; but knowing no object, and feeling no
care but to fpeculate and dream of vifionary
amendment, it confounded every thing with
an ignorant benevolence; and mixing the abufes
of power, with the hardfhips of the human lot
and exiftence, taught the people to throw off
with the refpect for their ancient inftitutions,
and eftablifhed government, every fanction of
morality, every paffive virtue; their fubmiffion
to the will of heaven, with that to the monarchy, and their religion together, with their al-
legiance.

One of the moft fublime and brilliant of thefe
delufive dreams, was what was called in the
lofty language of the revolution, the endlefs
*perfectibility* of the human fpecies* ; for fince
all its weaknefs, errors and calamities, were now
demonftrated to flow exclufively from evil governments, it followed that they would be cut
off in their fource and dried up for ever, by the
fimple inftitution of good ones ; if indeed, it
were not to be expected that fociety as it advanced towards perfection, would maintain
itfelf without government at all, by confent of
virtues, and uniformity of will.

* Condorcet, efquiffe d'un tableau hiftorique des progrès de
l'efpèce humaine, chap. dernier.

This principle, however, has been abandoned with the reft after a baneful experience. After having fwelled the vanity and inflamed the rancour of the people, after having caufed every fpecies of excellence to be confidered as an ufurpation and an injury, and levelled the ariftocracy of talents and virtues, with this of birth, and that of property, it is configned to oblivion— " We muft not, fays Lepeau* one of the kings whom the French have preferred to Louis the XVIth, we muft not make to ourfelves any chimerical idea of the perfection of man, he is nearly the fame at all times," a cruel fentence, remarkable for the coldnefs and phlegm with which it is delivered, but more remarkable for its infolence and falfhood, as he muft well know who has fo long fpeculated upon the ignorance and credulity, the paffions and prejudices of the people, and depraved and brutalized a whole nation, till it is become patient of him and his colleagues, after having murdered a prince, whofe only fault was to think it capable of virtue or amendment.

There remains therefore no danger from the brilliant chimeras, any more than from the vifi-

* Rapport au nom de la commiffion des onze.

ble

ble deformity of thofe principles which have defolated France. Not one of them has triumphed, and only one remains in exiftence. This one, however, contains the feeds of all the reft, for all would revive and fpring up again in foreign ftates, if France were permitted *to preferve her conquefts and deftroy the equilibrium of Europe.* Cured herfelf by experience, fhe would fpread around her the mifchiefs fhe banifhed from her own bofom, fhe would corrupt with the poifons fhe has vomited ; and, conquering with one hand and contaminating with the other, fhe would imprefs upon the nations that true diforganizing impulfe which would make them revolve for ever round her own endlefs revolutions.

But, though no principle of the revolution appears to have met with long fuccefs, or to be finally triumphant ; the acknowledgment of the republic, which is virtually made by his majefty's meffage of the 8th December ult. has been, I cannot perceive upon what grounds, interpreted by fome perfons, as a facrifice or humiliation upon the part of Great Britain. If it were fo, I profefs I think the time and circumftances under which it was made, namely, the bankruptcy of the enemy, and the fuceeffive defeats

and

and difafters they had encountered in Germany, the moft extraordinary that his fervants could have felected, for advifing him to any meafure unpleafant or derogatory to his feelings or pretenfions; I am inclined however to think, that there will be found confiderably more of magnanimity, than of mortification, in the language and fentiments of that meffage. Still it has been fufpected, that the adminiftration were adverfe to the acknowledgment of the republic, and therefore that this ftep is painful and humiliating to them. Upon this fubject, it is important to be explicit and perfpicuous, becaufe the opinion is capable of caufing much mifchief or delufion.

I have little doubt, then, that it would have been more fatisfactory to the feelings of the king's minifters, and to thofe of every honeft and fenfible mind in his majefty's dominions, if the fucceffes of this war had been fo general and complete on the one hand, and if the diftreffes and calamities of France on the other, had fo perfectly and effectually opened her eyes upon the inaptitude of a republican form of government to her phyfical and moral fituation, that the iffue of both combined fhould have been the reftoration of the monarchy; I fay, I have no doubt

doubt that fuch would have been their wifhes, as I have no fcruple to acknowledge that fuch are my own.—They include the return of the exiles, and a period to that mafs of individual mifery and perfecution, which is without a parallel in the hiftory of the world, unlefs perhaps in the fubverfion of the weftern empire, when whatever was civilized became the prey of whatever was barbarous; and an effeminate and diffolute world was plundered and oppreffed by a rude and favage race, that feemed frefh from nature, and vomited by the earth.

This, I think that they, and whoever can feel or reafon in thefe kingdoms, muft have defired with them—*Diis aliter vifum eft.* They have no power over fate, or controul upon neceffity; if they had, they would be fearfully refponfible for throwing away their arms, and acknowledging *even this* republic. Not that they, or the conftitution of this country, have any thing to apprehend, as I think it is infinuated, from its neighbourhood, or example. But that France herfelf has every thing to apprehend and to dread from it, but becaufe it is incompatible with the tranquillity and repofe of France herfelf, and becaufe the turbulence and revolutions of France are incompatible with the tranquillity and repofe of this country, and of Europe.

But

But we muſt not forget, or overlook, in the luſtre and dazzle of our own fortune and comparative proſperity, the *misfortunes of our allies* ; the ſpoliation and diſmemberment of Europe ; our own loſſes and privations; and, above all, the criminal danger of rejecting comparative good, for a ſpeculative and problematical better. —If, at this peace, we ſhall reinſtate them in all their poſſeſſions, reſtore the balance of Europe, and indemnify ourſelves, I proteſt, I ſhall never blame the government for acknowledging, nor apprehend any ſerious danger from the example of the tottering and deciduous republic they acknowledge.

I do not even admit, that the conſtitution of Great Britain would have any thing to apprehend from the eſtabliſhment of a republican form of government in France, though it were ſimple and perfect in its kind, and adjuſted to the ſoil, genius, manners, population, and extent of her territory, though, in one word it were fortunate and triumphant. I think the excellent modification of our conſtitution would not only reſiſt, but yield with ſecurity ; for two of its integral parts are already republican; and beſides this, it is peculiarly worthy of remark, that the municipal government of the kingdom is wholly and univerſally republican. If

If there could ever have exifted any danger
to the monarchical part of our conftitution,
from a comparifon of expence with the pretended cheapnefs of a republican form of government, which I am far from admitting, the prefent eftablifhments, and ftill more the fyftem
and principle of France, have totally removed
it. For though the malevolence of party may
have made the ignorant confider the whole of
the civil lift as an appanage of royalty ; though
the expences of the civil government, of the adminiftration of juftice, the falaries of the great
officers of ftate, the neceffary rewards or en-
couragements of talents and activity, and the
honourable relief of the meritorious and unhappy, are carefully forgotten whenever the
civil lift is founded in the ears of the people, yet
the people cannot fail to difcover, that under
whatever form the public impofitions are levied,
or to whatever direction they are nominally attributed, that government muft, in fact, be
maintained at the cheapeft expence, which exacts the fmalleft contributions from their purfes.
When they fee, therefore, a republican tax-
gatherer bearing off cloth or corn to a republican warehoufe ; or read a republican law for
enabling the people to fell their furniture, in
order to pay their quota of a forced loan to a
republican government, and for imprifoning a

I                          dilatory

dilatory republican lender, they will eafily infer
that their own government is in effect cheaper,
if it were only becaufe they need not give their
fhoes to the army, nor put their beds up to fale,
in order to avoid the jail, or the fcaffold, which
fill up the back ground of this horrible picture.

But if thefe atrocious cruelties and extortions
were to difappear at the period of returning
peace, there would ftill arife out of the ftate
and extravagance of the directory, and the
number of their officers and affiftants, out of
more than forty thoufand diftinct adminiftra-
tions, maintained and paid by the indivifible republic, out of the falaries of the members of
both houfes of the French parliament, and the
innumerable millions delivered to the fecret dif-
cretion of the feveral minifters, which form a
part of *the civil lift of the republic*, a comparifon too prominent and glaring, to leave any
thing to be apprehended for the decent magni-
ficence of the monarchy of England.

One danger, however, and by no means a
trivial and light one, will arife from the eftablifhment of the actual republic we difcover in
France : not, indeed, from its excellency or fuperiority over our own conftitution, but from
its confcious inferiority and feeblenefs, which
there is reafon to fear may incline it to feek a
fpecies

fpecies of fafety in the commotions and difturbances of foreign countries.

A bad government is always a bad neigh-
bour ; and we have four years of uninterrupted
experience that it is fo : but a bad government,
ingrafted upon the reftlefs character of a ruined
and corrupted people, is the worft and moft
dangerous of all ; and the *irruption* that may be
expected, immediately after the peace, from
that country, is not the leaft or lighteft of the
evils for which his majefty's minifters may have
to devife a remedy or an antidote.

If this republic, however, is to be confidered
as a wife, falutary, and durable inftitution, calculated for the happinefs of France, and capable
of giving tranquillity to Europe, it will remain
impoffible, under that point of view, to difcover
any thing in agreeing to it, which ought to be
repugnant or humiliating to the feelings of his
majefty's fervants. But if it is even now tottering towards change or diffolution, as I confefs it is my own individual belief and opinion,
and is only fo far calculated to reftore peace and
reft to the bofom of that criminal and bleeding
country, as it is the intermediate and prepara-
tory ftep to the reftoration of monarchy, and of
the antient fundamental laws and government
of the land ; if all that is eftimable, or even
pardonable in it, is the public abjuration of pure

and

unqualified democracy; and the fpectacle of
rank, gradation, and authority, once more re-
prefented and rendered familiar to the people.—
If this is the true light and colour in which it
ought to be beheld, then I imagine *a-fortiori*,
that no man will be bold or perfidious enough
to affert, that they have departed or abandoned
any part of their object, fo far as the reftoration
of a rational government to France, might have
entered into their confideration, as one of the
refults of a favourable iffue of the war. I think,
on the contrary, that as the war was not carried
on for the attainment of this object, though
circumftances foon pointed it out as one of the
beft means both of terminating the quarrel with
celerity, and fixing the peace upon the true and
folid bafis of reciprocal advantage and fecurity,
the minifters could never in any cafe, even in
that of complete difcomfiture and failure, have
been thought to have abandoned, or yielded any
condition which they were bound to obtain by
any fpecies of engagement whatfoever; and that
having arrived at a point at which the power
and the refources of the enemy are no longer
formidable, and from which it is reafonable to
forefee, and prefume ftill further returns towards the eftablifhment of a mixed and practicable conftitution, it would, in any view of
the cafe, be cruel and wrong to continue the

war upon that account, or to exact, at the
fword's point, the exprefs ftipulation of things
which they never affumed the right to prefcribe,
but which they have reafon to expect from the
reftoration of peace and from the prefent condition of France.

Under thefe circumftances, we find ourfelves
in a fituation and capacity to negociate, and the
king's meffage to parliament, *December* 8, 1795,
has effectually removed any opinion which might
have been entertained of a difinclination in his
majefty's fervants to treat with the executive
directory of France. All difficulties in the way
to peace have been effectually removed, on the
part of Great Britain, and the war, being reduced to the fimple and ordinary nature of all
former contefts, would inftantly determine, if
the French government could be induced, either
by the fenfe of the internal mifery and calamities
of the people, or by the defpair of creating any
domeftic difturbances in England, to depart
from the decree of *September* 30, 1795, and
abandon the *exterior principle*, as they have done
every other principle of the revolution.

Their obftinacy upon this article may, perhaps, have been confiderably impaired by the
recent and important fucceffes of the Auftrian
arms, by the vifible approach of bankruptcy
and famine, and by the difappointment of any
expectations they might have entertained of a
political

political explofion in this country. They muft
have remarked, in the firft place, the univerfal
fenfe of the kingdom, moft unequivocally declared in fo many addreffes to the throne and to
the parliament; they muft have obferved the
refults of a profperity, hitherto unknown and
incredible, during three years of the moft violent and univerfal hoftility, in which their own
country has been completely exhaufted of all its
means and refources; the high value of the public funds, the competition for the loan, and the
unhoped-for lightnefs of the new taxes, cannot
have efcaped their attention; they muft have feen,
that not a fingle article of neceffity is comprized
in them, at a time that their own laft defperate
remedy confifts only in the hope of laying hands
upon every article of neceffity, by a forcible levy
of them from the feveral proprietors in kind.

And if they cannot fail to make this humiliating comparifon at home, I would afk what
confolation they can derive from enlarging their
profpeƈt, and bringing the whole theatre of the
war under their contemplation. I forbear to
enumerate thefe circumftances, which are dif-
treffing and difaftrous; it is better to confider
France upon that fide where fhe counts her acquifitions, and paffes for profperous and triumphant.

I was always of opinion that her conquefts
would

would be burthenfome to her during the war, notwithftanding the temporary relief and affift-ance fhe might draw from them by her requifi-tions and forcible contributions ; and as it be-comes evident that fhe cannot retain them at the general peace, it is probable that fhe would inftantly withdraw her armies from the greateft part of them, if fhe did not expect to make ad-vantage of them in the negociation, by exacting conceffions, in the nature of an equivalent, from Great Britain ; in every other point of view, they have certainly been hurtful to her, if any thing is finally to be confidered in that light which has accelerated the period of pacification, by extending and attenuating her efforts, in the fame proportion that they diverted and exhaufted her means and refources. But fhe can never forget that, by the conqueft of Holland, fhe made a direct prefent to England of the Cape of Good Hope and Ceylon, probably of Batavia, and all the Dutch colonies, which would be an immenfe fource of commercial wealth and ag-grandizement to that power, even during the war, if it were to continue; whereas all the advantage fhe could expect from the occupation of the Dutch territory in Europe, deprived and cut off from its dependencies, refolved itfelf into a reverfion and fpeculation of profit fubfequent to the peace.

In

In the Netherlands the conduct of France affords a more unequivocal proof that she never dreamed of preferving them; becaufe fhc reduced her whole views to the ufufruct or wafte of the moment, ranfoming the inhabitants, and exporting every thing even to the tools of induftry and materials of agriculture; in the fame manner, finding it impoffible to retain her colonies in the Weft-Indies, fhe endeavoured, in the language of the revolution, to *neutralize* or render them unprofitable to whatever ftate might acquire them. Here, befides the natural ruin of thofe beautiful plantations, and the free fcope fhe gave to fire and deftruction, fhe unchained a fpirit, which I fear will be found too ftrong and powerful for the arts or arms of all Europe to fubdue. Not contented with the fpoil and havoc of her own unfortunate iflands, fhe extended her atrocious policy to the colonies of England, and endeavoured to lay the foundations of a negro empire in the weftern Archipelago. It is not neceffary to the fubject I am treating, that I fhould enquire, with any degree of minutenefs, into the degree of her fuccefs, or the poffibility of devifing a remedy; it is fufficient that the fyftem of wafte and deftruction fhe purfued fhould eftablifh the fact, that fhe never expected to retain thefe poffeffions at the peace; and that it has fuccceded, fo far at leaft as to render them

of

of very inferior value to whatever power may be
fuppofed likely to acquire them; not only Marti-
nico, for inftance, and the other iflands, which
I take for granted fhe is ready to furrender, are
diminifhed in their value and fecurity, but many
of our own fettlements have been almoft equally
deftroyed and corrupted; fo that it may ferioufly
be doubted, in the prefent circumftances, whether thofe parts of the world have not loft, at
leaft for a very long time to come, the greateft
part of their original value, and confequently
whether they contain the juft confideration and
materials of any equivalent whatfoever.

But I know not, I confefs, under what tenure or fecurity, fhort of the abfolute union of
of them all under one and the fame metropoli-
tan power, they are likely to be retained, or to
exift. There muft not, I think, be an *analogy*,
but an identity of government, if they are to remain the property of any of the ftates of Europe; for I cannot perceive any profpect, or entertain the fhadow of an hope that France, at
any future period of time, fhould be inclined
to prefer the prefervation of thofe colonies which
might be left to her at the peace, to the deftruction of ours, which would always remain at
her mercy, if we were to hold them by no better tenure than an *analogy* between the governments: particularly if it were fo to happen, that

K                                   we

we were understood to receive out of these colonies any confiderable part of our indemnity for the expences of the war, and of our equivalent for her own acquifitions in Europe. How fmall would be the direct and pofitive intereft of France, in her circumfcribed and diminifhed plantations, how fubordinate and fecondary to that abominable delight fhe might take in inflicting the fevereft wounds upon her rival, with fo little prejudice and danger to herfelf? ·

If the retaining, befides, of our colonies, is to depend upon an analogy in the refpective governments, that analogy muft make one of the reciprocal conditions in the articles of peace, and will depend upon the obfervation of a treaty, which it will be the intereft of one of the contracting parties to violate.—For the performance of fuch ftipulations, I apprehend no other fecurity can poffibly be devifed, than an equality and reciprocity of intereft in our common poffeffions. But this would reduce us, in that part of the world, very nearly to the *ftatus quo* before the war, and preclude us from all poffibility of finding indemnity or equivalent in the Weft Indies.

While I am upon this fubject of *equivalent,* and to prevent the neceffity of returning to it in another piace, I fhall take the opportunity of confeffing, that I am aware of no circumftances,

ftances, under the actual or relative fituation of the contending parties; which ought to call this fubject into difcuffion at all. I think it is incompatible with the honour of Great Britain; her engagements with her allies, and the peace and independence of Europe, of which fhe is the protector and guarantee, to admit it at all into deliberation; and that no peace, which can embrace thefe interefts and duties, can be negociated upon any other footing than the *ftatus quo ante bellum*, with fuch indemnities to Great Britain as fhe is entitled to by the events of the war.

It is the general fyftem and balance of power, for which we are contending, (though perhaps, if it is poffible, ftill dearer and nearer interefts are involved in it) it is the independence of this great commonwealth of Europe, which our arms have vindicated and afferted; and I will never admit any bafis of peace, which fhould abandon, or compromife, or expofe it. Much lefs could I bring myfelf to behold with temper or forbearance, the fpectacle of the two great powers, which have attacked and defended its liberties, rearing the altar of peace upon its cinders, and dividing the fpoil and plunder with a common violence, but an unequal depravity. For France would be guilty only of a crime of force, which would come home laden to the

bofom

bofom of Great Britain, with all the accumulated guilt of fraud, treachery, and perfidioufnefs.

When I fpeak of the *ftatus quo ante bellum*, it cannot be fuppofed that, after fo many violent fhocks and convulfions, it can be replaced exactly, and in all its parts, upon its former foundations; or that every local variation which may have taken place, every change of conftitution, or of foreign connexions, is a juft caufe for continuing the war. Thofe countries, in particular, which have not been true to their own caufe, whofe cowardice, indifference, or treachery, is the fource of their actual derangement, cannot expect their internal interefts to be adopted by the generality of Europe, after the firft poffibility of fecuring the common independence by a juft and fecure pacification. Every thing local, every perfonal intereft muft difappear before this great and imperious neceffity : a barrier muft be provided againft the unconquerable fpirit of ufurpation, and the natural predominance of France. Of this every ftate is convinced by a fearful experience ; the emperor, in particular, who will poffefs thofe fertile and populous provinces, by an uncertain and precarious tenure, as long as they lie open to the firft incurfions of the republic, will haften to repair the errors of Jofeph the Second, and reftore the defences of the Netherlands. The

other

other provinces of the Low Countries, to whofe
diforders I have alluded, if they do not fhake off,
by their own efforts, the yoke of the fatal con-
nexion they have formed with fo much cowardice and criminality, will thus at leaft be rendered an inferior and lefs dangerous acquifition
to the ufurper; and at any rate, the liberties
and independence of Europe may yet be defended
in another war, inftead of being liable to be
overwhelmed by the firft armed emigrations of
Frenchmen !

There is another circumftance which can
fcarcely efcape the obfervation of France, namely, that notwithftanding the facility with which
the loan has been made, and the lightnefs of
the taxes, we have confiderably diminifhed our
eftablifhments and reduced the expences, by
circumfcribing the operations of the war. She
muft have obferved in the eftimates for the current year a reduction of 800,000l. fterling, in
the army alone : and if fhe ftill cherifhes any hope
of infurrection, fhe muft obferve, that, "by the
recalling of all our forces from the continent, it
is fcarcely poffible for any of her friends to recommend that meafure to the public as *prudent*,
under our actual circumftances and fituation.

If fhe entertains any fanguine expectation
from the dreadful vifitation of fcarcity, fhe cannot poffibly forget to obferve, that this danger

is

is common to both countries, and nearer and greater in her own; and that if there is a period before us, when fhe might take advantage of our languor and debility, it can only be upon the fuppofition that fhe herfelf fhould remain in health and vigour: all our privations and fufferings will avail her nothing, while her own are more poignant and unendurable. The carcafe of France cannot come to infult the ficknefs of Great Britain.

But I cannot apprehend that fhe will ever ferioufly rely for any hope of extrication from her prefent calamities, upon the uneafinefs and impatience of this country under its own. Not only becaufe fhe muft ftarve while we are upon allowance, but becaufe the war is perhaps favourable to England in this particular, in the fame degree as it is ruinous to France, by fhutting her from the granaries, or intercepting the eommerce of America, the Baltic, and the Mediterranean. Thefe markets are all open to England, but as foon as peace arrives, if the fcarcity were to continue, fhe would meet a French commiffary in every one of them, whom the greater neceffities of his country would compel to outbid her every where, or at leaft to advance the price to an enormous and incalculable increafe.

The corn trade, at different periods of the

war,

war, has been permitted and denied to France
by our fleets, which actually formed the block-
ade of that country ; independently of any reafons which might arife from general laws and
ufage, from particular treaties, or policy refpecting neutral powers, it might be difficult
to determine which of the alternatives, adopted
at the different times I have mentioned, was
the moft wife and advantageous to Great Britain ; for, though her enemy has doubtlefs
fuffered many partial inconveniences and difafters by her captures, I think a more general and
univerfal wound has been inflicted by the avarice and extortion of the neutral powers, and
the interefted affiftance they have been permitted to lend her.

It appears certain, that not only the cargoes,
freight, and infurance were regularly paid for
in fpecie by the French confuls or commiffa-
ries, in the neutral countries, before the veffels
proceeded, but that a depofit was exacted equal
to the value of the fhip's bottom, in cafe of
capture or fhipwreck, and of detention in the
French ports : for the government was often
unable to reftrain the violence of the populace,
and frequently, before thefe precautions, obliged, by its own neceffities, to take fimilar liberties with the property of its good friends and
allies.

It

It is almoſt ſuperfluous to remark, how violently ſuch a commerce muſt have drained the precious metals out of France *.— The ſpecie of that country, from the conſequences of emigration, and, probably, from the precaution and ſpeculations of thoſe who have not emigrated, had long ſince begun to ooze into all the countries of Europe ; her armies, and the hazardous traffic ſhe was forced to ſubmit to for their maintenance, opened the dykes ſtill wider, and the torrent has flowed without reflux or relaxation.

If I were enquiring into the cauſes of the total diſappearance of the precious metals in that country, I ſhould not forget to mention that maſs of them which has returned into the bowels of the earth, which fear and danger have ingeniouſly concealed, which has been buried by hands now buried, and in places guarded by the ſilence of oblivion, and the ſecrecy of the tomb. But I am deſirous only of

---

* Eſchaſſeriaux, in his celebrated report of the 22d Brumaire, upon the ſtate of the finances, aſſigns as a principal cauſe of their diſorder, " des approviſionnemens immenſes de ſubſiſtances, &c. achetés chez l'étranger pour remplir le gouffre dévorant de nos beſoins." He ſays afterwards that " nos rélations extérieures ont été ruineuſes par le bouleverſement du change, & par les efforts de l'étranger pour nous le rendre défavorable, &c." Same report.

remarking,

remarking, that part of her treafure, which has paffed her frontier, and carried itfelf into other ftates, becaufe I fufpect, that, by the effect of the revolution in Holland, and other circum-ftances, it has principally concentered itfelf in England, and is no fmall caufe of that enor-mous depreciation of the value of money, which is the counterfign of a dearnefs of commodities, and gives the furface and appearance of a real fcarcity and want.

It is not my defign to encourage any idea that may have been entertained of exaggeration in the deficiency of the late harvefts, from the intereftednefs and fpeculation of individuals. Such an opinion, though perhaps not wholly unfounded, it would be exceedingly dangerous to act upon, and to maintain the confumption in confequence, at its ufual proportions, becaufe an error in our calculation would infallibly conduct us to a fudden and abfolute privation ; but I think it material to obferve the fall in the value of money, which makes a part of the apparent fcarcity of corn, as well as of the imputed dear-nefs of every other article of neceffity or con-venience.

France, however, muft perceive that the fcar-city in England, though exaggerated by male-volence, and affigned by ignorance exclufively to the war, is in fome degree the refult of the

national

national profperity, of a redundancy in the
quantity of the precious metals, which, aug-
mented by the high credit of paper, and the
opinion both of public and perfonal folvency,
France muft difcern that it arifes in part from
the fudden influx of her own fpecie, from the
balance of our favourable commerce with the
whole world, and from our becoming the exchange, or bank, of fo great a part of it ; and
what muft be more painful and difcouraging to
her, after being difappointed in her hope of infurrections, from the momentary inconvenien-
cies to which this decreafe in the value of money has fubjected a part of the people, fhe muft
obferve, that the proportion between the public
debt and the national revenues is diminifhed and
reduced by it. And if fhe could not behold the
effect of the fyftem eftablifhed in 1786, and the
provifion for paying one per cent. intereft out
of the taxes themfelves impofed during the war,
without concern and aftonifhment, with what
fentiments muft fhe fee the filent and progreffive operation of this important caufe, which,
while labour and wages re-eftablifh their natural and indifpenfible level, will give frefh vigour and activity to induftry and commerce, ·
which operates as a direct tax upon the metals
themfelves, which falls with invariable juftice,
and even accuracy, upon every clafs and proportion

portion of capital, while it diminifhes the mortgage of the country, and the whole mafs of its
debt, which no longer reprefent the fame portion of its annual produce or induftry?

I now come to fpeak of the principal ob-
ftacles of peace, as they appear to me at this
moment, a fubject which I confider as exceedingly important to be fo far explained to the
public, as is confiftent with political prudence;
and that neceffary liberty, in negotiation, which
makes it impoffible for the King's fervants to
unfold themfelves either with much latitude or
with much precifion.

*Peace*, it is to be obferved, often chaced from
the earth by the paffions and follies of men, is
not to be won back by the firft vows of returning moderation and wifdom. If it is fometimes
exiled by crime and ambition, it does not always
return with reafon and humanity. Such, I
think, is the fituation of the world at this con-
juncture; fo great and general the experience
and wearinefs of the ills of war, that *with the
exception of a fmall band of intriguers and politicians*, peace is the univerfal hope, defire, and
prayer of all the nations of Europe. Twenty
millions of individuals invite peace daily back to
France, with the piercing cries of mifery, oppreffion, and famine, which peace alone can
relieve, and which neither the fraud nor the

terror

terror of the government can ftifle or fupprefs.
The territories of ftrangers offer the fame vows
from another defcription of her miferable people,
with the fpectacle of whofe wrongs and fufferings every part of the world is filled and pol-
luted : a profcribed and devoted clafs, whofe
extremes of fortune have rendered them fo interefting to the natural fenfiblity and unconquerable prejudices of mankind, and who expect
in peace, a period at leaft to the cruel hope
which devours them. Peace, too, is equally defired by the enemies of France, and by thofe
ftates which fhe holds by violence, or defolates
with her perfidious fraternity. The magnanimity of Great Britain invokes peace with public
vows, in which the proud mifery of the government of France refufes to join. The emperor
courts peace even under the mediation of a
power but too friendly to France : the *poffible*
mediation of Spain is intercepted by the profef-
fion of pretenfions fo lofty and ridiculous, fo
vain and prepofterous, that it is impoffible not
to perceive that thefe men are not only enemies
to peace, but to the very name of it. Preffed
to it at home by the voice, or rather by the
fhrieks and fcreams of the people, courted to it
abroad by nations friendly or neutral, as well as
by thofe which have felt the common calamity
of war, and fo naturally defire to return to tranquillity,

quillity, they are not afraid of oppofing their un-
attainable ambition to the common prayers and
common neceffities of Europe.

As it appears now certain, from whatever
caufe, that the perfons poffeffed of authority in
France are averfe to peace, and that they have
no means of carrying on the war, but thofe
which were employed by the committees of
Robefpierre, it becomes important to enquire
how far the renovation of the reign of terror
might operate in this country as an obftacle to
pacification. There can be no doubt that a government founded upon thefe cruel and abominable principles, affords to every other a juft
and honourable excufe for infulating it amidft
the ftates of Europe, and refufing to hold any
intercourfe or communion with it; and as we
already perceive this atrocious fyftem rearing itfelf upon the ruins of the conftitution of 1795,
it appears to me to be entitled to a confiderable
degree of attention and reflexion, how far it may
be wife, or confiftent with our former declara-
tions, to treat at this time with the French nation, fhould it prove unable to maintain that
conftitution, and relapfe into all the crimes and
horrors from which it feemed to have emerged
upon the ninth of Thermidor.

In the firft place, I fhould imagine this fyftem is incapable of becoming permanent; and
that,

that, during its energy, it muſt more quickly
empty and exhauſt the country, than could be
accompliſhed by any weaker principle, or inferior degree of violence and deſolation : conſequently, that France will arrive ſooner at that
point of depreſſion and debility, beyond which
ſhe cannot puſh, and before which ſhe will not
check her deſperate career. In this point of
view, it ſeems by no means certain that the return of *terroriſm* will retard the epoch of peace.
But it may be thought that it will at leaſt reſtore the materials of war, and enable the government of France to renew thoſe extraordinary efforts under the firſt ſhock of which the
whole continent of Europe has been ſo nearly
cruſhed or overwhelmed. I am not, I confeſs,
of this opinion ; I do not entertain even this ap-
prehenſion in my boſom. The whole internal
ſtate of France aſſures me that this fear is viſi-
onary, or at leaſt ſuperfluous and vain. The
mighty chaſms that defeat, deſertion, diſaffec-
tion, and the ſcaffold, have made in the French
nation, cannot be ſo ſoon filled up ; their armies
cannot be recruited from thoſe depopulated
towns which they have filled with military maſ-
ſacres, and the very ſtones of which they have
levelled with the earth. By the fiſcal ſyſtem of
· Robeſpierre, every capitaliſt was plundered ; and
if it were only from the diſperſion of the ſame
quantity

quantity of fpecie into a greater number of hands,
it will not be fo eafy for the guillotine to reple-
nifh the exchequer. In his time, and for him, the
wifh of Caligula feemed to have been realized,
and the whole nation to have but one neck and
one executioner; the prefent government will be
forced to all the details of violence and murder,
to difcriminate and diftinguifh at leaft, becaufe
it muft opprefs more than one clafs, and profcribes
thofe who have the revolutionary merit of having profcribed fo many others. In truth, I am
not able to perceive the rich or the riches of
France; let the directory, wring a cancelled
and ufelefs paper from the vile hands enriched
by the revolution, will it pay the neutral powers
who have exhaufted the whole fpecie of the
empire, and procure from them frefh fuel and
materials of war ? I do not think it ; but it will
tear from every proprietor, in every part of
France, his particular poffeffion, and accumu-
late every natural production or article of manu-
facture in the warehoufes of the government.
This point I have already treated; it remains
for me only to obferve, that the fuccefs muft
be various, as the tyranny is more or lefs in-
tenfe, as the public fpirit, and the human fpirit, are more or lefs extinct or torpid in the
different departments and dependencies, as the
ruin of agriculture and induftry is more or lefs
accomplifhed,

accomplifhed, as the deftruction of the cities is more perfect or incomplete.

For thefe reafons, I am not inclined to appre- hend fo much from this fyftem even during hoftilities; and at the peace, I think it will re- pofe in the common tomb of every forced and unnatural principle, with the reft of the mif- fhapen progeny of the revolution. During the war, it will grow weak with the weaknefs of the country upon which it preys, and confume itfelf with the materials it devours. If it rages with equal violence, it will be confined to fewer and diminifhing objects, the moral evil muft languifh with the natural infirmity, or when the body is emaciated and bed-ridden, there will at leaft be little to dread from the idle frenzy of the brain, though it fancy the poor machine it wears and agitates a hero or a god, unconquered or unconquerable.

The prevalence, I confefs, of the fame fyf- tem in 1796 would not with me be fo material an obftacle to peace as it was in 1794, becaufe the madnefs of a cripple is not fo formidable as that of a giant; the danger, befides, of every principle is proportioned to the force and power that fupport it, and the final triumph and fuc- cefs that it obtains; in this point of view, there- fore, it certainly cannot be dangerous to nego- tiate; and I fhould incline to think that it is

not

not contradictory to the fpirit of any of our de-
clarations, becaufe the danger and contagion of
principles diminifhing with the force that main-
tains them, it cannot be their abftract exiftence
againft which we are at war, or which forms
an obftacle to peace, but the degree of credit
and authority they poffefs, and the phyfical
power they animate and direct; as thefe therefore have decayed and declined, and promife
quickly to expire, I am not able to perceive any
inconfiftency between our conduct and our pro-
feffions, even though we fhould treat with
France under the influence of that deteftable,
but now impotent fyftem.

It is a reflection painful and degrading to humanity, that a handful of ftupid and brutal ty-
rants, juft efcaped from the fetters of Robefpierre, fhould have been able to rivet them
upon twenty millions of beings, and with their
own necks fmoking and fcarred with that oppro-
brious yoke, enflave and bind fo vaft a population
in chains, almoft heavier than thofe they themfelves had worn. That a contemptible band, whofe
little finger is heavier than the loins of Richlieu
and Mazarine, with their forced loan, their taxes
in kind, their requifitions, and their maximum,
that is to fay, by public plunder and public terror, fpeculating upon the cowardice and torpor
of the human fpecies, fhould be able to prolong

M                                    and

and redouble all the miferies of France, involve fo many other ftates in protracted danger and calamities, and prevent any fettlement or fyftem being reftored or eftablifhed in Europe.—It is a reflection ftill more degrading, ftill more infulting, ftill more cruel, that thefe men fhould rely for fuccefs or impunity, not only on the depravity of their own *fubjects*, but on ours ; not upon the abject and paffive character, which four years of fuccefsful cruelty and crimes have impreffed upon Frenchmen, but upon I know not what activity and alacrity in treafon and revolt, which they prefume in Great Britain.

The firft obftacle to peace, therefore, that I can perceive on the part of France, is the unqualified ambition of the *government* ; which, in fpite of their own neceffities, or the inhuman alternatives of oppreffion, which alone remain to them, is determined to maintain the decrees for incorporating the conquefts ; a determination of which it is impoffible to doubt, as far as depends upon them, fince their rejection of the mediation of the Court of Denmark, and the internal meafures of violence and defperation to which they have reforted in order to be able to carry on the war for another campaign.

Into

Into the caufes of this refolution on their part
it is very material to inquire; becaufe we know
by repeated or rather continued and invariable
experience, that refolutions and decrees, and
even fundamental articles of the conftitution,
are but a dead letter fo foon as they ceafe to co-
incide with the wifhes or interefts of the perfons who ought to be bound by them. The
caufes do not arife folely in the ambition, but
grow out of the danger and embarraffments of
the government. To difband their fourteen armies at once, might neither be fafe for themfelves, nor contribute to the internal tranquillity
of a country which has long known no law but
force, no morality but fubmiffion. Crimes
are become mechanical in France, and five hundred thoufand inftruments no longer obedi-
ent to the fame impulfe, might fall into collifion
with each other, or tear the ill-jointed fabric of
government into pieces. Peace too, without
fome order in the finances, without fome revi-
vification of the marine and of commerce, without the reftoration of agriculture, or the fettlement of property, (which I think can never
take place fo long as a fingle affignat remains in
exiftence) without manufactures, without induftry, without religion, without morals:—Peace,
I fay, without all thefe, may not be very defira-
ble, may appear even dangerous, to men who
have not the means of bringing back their coun-

trymen

trymen to order and peaceful arts, to honeft and
domeftic duties, to the intercourfe and habits of
civilized life and fociety.

Peace, however, is neceffary to France, becaufe the armies that devour her demand peace
themfelves, and cannot be maintained without
the repetition of thofe violent meafures that
make peace demanded by the people: without
redoubling thofe oppreffions which muft finally
produce fome explofion too violent for the government to conduct or refift; an explofion
which, moft probably, is only fufpended and
delayed from the hope of being anticipated by
fimilar calamities in London. France, has no better title to rely upon the fpirit of infurrection than
upon the eforts of the fcarcity, nor can I think
the government fincere in this expectation, however convenient it might be to their own wifhes
and exigencies, as well as thofe of the nation.
Still it muft be confeffed, that the difturbances in
London, however infignificant, the coalition of
the clubs with the oppofition in parliament, and
the violent doctrines of fome of their leaders, to
which I have already alluded, with the fubfequent
affociations recommended by perfons of confequence in the Whig club, have been particularly
favourable, if not to the encouragement of
that hope in the government of France, at leaft
to the propagation of it, and the confequent delufion of the people. To this, I imagine, is in
fome

fome degree to be attributed the apparent indifference with which the king's communication
to parliament has been received at Paris; becaufe, fuppofing the probability of infurrections
in this country, it was not impoffible to attribute the conciliating nature of that meffage to
the apprehenfions of the minifters, and to make
it be believed, that even this meafure was an in-
dication of the approach of the commotions they
expected.

I have faid, I did not think the government
of Paris was the dupe of the expectation they
fpread abroad, nor of the appearances of difturbances in England, with which they nourifhed
the belief of it, and I will now ftate my reafons
for entertaining that opinion. It could not have
efcaped the penetration, one would imagine, of
the executive directory, the minifters, and the
two counfels of the legiflature, that the nature
and temper of our parties are extremely diffimi-
lar and diftinct from their own violent and fpeculative divifions; that no alterations in the conftitution, and in the government, no change,
but a change of perfons, could be ferioufly intended by the oppofition; they muft before this
time have difcovered, that the alliance of great
peers and proprietors would moderate the eccen-
tricity, if it added to the confiftency of the focieties, and abridge or diminifh the velocity of
their

their movement by the very weight and folidity it added to them; they muſt know, beſides, that they could have but little aſſiſtance to expect from the union of two deſcriptions of perſons, whoſe oppoſite principles, and contending inte-reſts, were an inſuperable bar to the ſincerity or duration of the contract; that it was founded upon mutual fraud and deception ; and that the conditions of the alliance were a term, at which the one would never be contented to ſtop, and where the other would never be willing to ar-rive.

Certainly, through whatever medium this tranſaction may be conſidered in France, where there is an intereſt to colour and diſtort it, it requires no very great degree of perſpicacity or clear ſightedneſs to diſtinguiſh here, that no danger can poſſibly ariſe from it to the govern-ment or conſtitution. I mean during its leaſe and continuance ; for at the moment of its diſ-ſolution, a real peril will ariſe, but which, I hope, may be as effectually guarded againſt, as it is eaſily foreſeen. If the oppoſition, for in-ſtance, ſhould prove the dupe in this compcti-tion of fraud and duplicity, inſtead of the ſocie-ties; if it ſhould finally appear, by a critical ex-periment, that the new leaders, inſtead of creat-ing a force which they are able to regulate and controul, ſhall have organized a power too fu-

rious

rious for their government, and for that of the country, (the common error and mifcalculation of fanguine and difappointed ambition) then there will arife a ferious and imminent danger indeed ; a danger not peculiar to the king's minifters and fervants, but broad and general, common to every clafs and defcription of men, though nearer to thefe very leaders, as they may read in the fate of Orleans and Rochefoucault, a double monument of miftaken probity and perfifting depravity; a common mirror to interefted vice and fpeculative virtue.

Suppofing, however, that I am miftaken in my conjecture of the effect this coalition, (coupled with the doctrines of a paffive refiftance and a prudential revolt, which followed clofe upon it) may operate upon the opinion of the government in France, and that they fhould be inclined to confider the occafion as favourable to their long-fufpended, but favourite plan of *invafion:* for I wifh to diffemble no fpecies of danger or inconvenience which can poffibly refult from the continuance of the war, and I think every thing poffible, both to defpair and to enthufiafm : I am fo far from apprehending that they would derive any affiftance from this coalition in that cafe, that I am perfuaded it would be the precife caufe of its immediate diffolution. Befides that they would meet great, and I think, infurmountable

infurmountable difficulties upon the fea, and even before they could afcend upon it; they would not find the moment particularly opportune or propitious, when the kingdom is full of difciplined and experienced troops, and of militia and provincial forces, that may be compared with them in almoſt every refpect, without injury or difparagement. They cannot be ignorant, that the dangers of England have always united all her parties ; they cannot think oppofition more formidable to government at this crifis, than when half the prefent fervants of his majeſty were to be numbered with it; nor forget, that thofe very dangers were the caufe of giving ſo much weight and confiſtency to adminiſtration, by withdrawing the moſt powerful and reſpectable individuals from the midſt of it.

For my own part, I confeſs, that it has fallen to my lot to know the opinion pretty generally entertained in foreign countries of the corruption and depravity of our parties, and to know that it is exaggerated and miſtaken. There is ſomething in our national character and difpofition, which commonly corrects and qualifies the vileſt paſſions and tendencies, and extracts or tempers the worſt poifons that circulate in our blood. Faction and civil war itfelf, have been found temperate evils in this climate

to

to what they have proved under other Ikies; and the experience we have had of them, has enabled us to prepare and provide from afar, againſt their return or contagion. If we except the rebellions, on account of the diſputed ſucceſſion, which aroſe from a falſe fenſe of honour and a miſtaken duty, the whole empire, ſince the period of the revolution, has been united upon every occafion of danger or neceſſity, and no part or party can claim any merit in this refpect, or pre-eminence over the reſt; we are loud and noiſy in the out-poſts, but when the body of the place is attacked or expoſed, we forget our divifions, and form the common garriſon of our country.

Neither can it have eſcaped, I imagine, the penetration of the French miniſtry, that the harangues and motions of the oppofition for peace, are not more likely to be fincere, than they are to prevail; for they, no doubt, whatever we may do at home, confider an oppofition as a *poſſible adminiſtration*, and enquire not only into what they ſay, but what they would do, and what they muſt do, if they were truſted with the government. They may poſſibly believe, that if Mr. Fox had been in power at the beginning of the year 1793, he would have ſent an ambaſſador to demand reparation for the violation of the treaties : they may poſſibly believe,

N     that

that he might have diffembled his horror at the
murder of the royal family, and accepted fatis-
faction for the confpiracy into which the convention had entered with our own traitors, to
fubvert the throne and the conftitution: they may
believe it poffible, that if Mr. Fox had been minifter, the war might have broken out fix
months later; or to fet no limits to credulity,
they might believe, that if Mr. Fox had been
minifter, we fhould ftill have been at peace;
—But if they had faith for all this; if
they could fubmit their reafon to all thefe
dogmas of oppofition, it would not follow that
they fhould believe alfo, that if Mr. Fox were
the minifter in 1796, after the contrary of all
thefe fuppofitions had taken place, he would
fubmit to the decree of the convention, and dif-
mantle the fleets of England, while France in-
corporated Savoy, the Netherlands, and all the
left bank of the Rhine. They need not believe,
becaufe Mr. Fox had once wifhed for peace,
that he would therefore throw away all the advantages of war; that he would forget the victory of the firft of June 1794, or the deftruction
of half the French navy in the harbours of
Toulon; they would not believe that Mr. Fox,
any more than Mr. Pitt, or any one Englifhman
more than another, would fubmit to the preliminaries they exact, or come to a negotiation
till France had repealed her decree; nay, I will

go further, becaufe it is neceffary to expofe
fully the expectations and reliances of that government; and I will fay, that if that decree
had been any thing elfe, in their own eftimation,
than an obftacle and barrier to every fpecies of
negotiation, which, of all things is uppermoft
in their apprehenfion, they would never have
fuffered it to pafs, or would have repealed it
with a precipitation greater than that with
which they paffed it : for, if the ftate of the
nations at war had been reverfed, and, inftead
of France, England had been ruined and exhaufted; if there were no power in Europe
upon foot to reprefs the ufurpations of France,
and it were clear that fhe muft, *de facto*, ex-
tend herfelf to the Rhine, what would be the
end or advantage of maintaining this proud and
vain-glorious decree?—Would it not rather remove the term, and endanger the event of that
ambitious peace, which fhe would otherwife
have the certainty of concluding, by humiliating and exafperating her enemies, by driving
them to incalculable efforts of thoughtlefs and
unmeafurable defpair? Can they think, then,
that England, entire and untouched, will
crouch to thofe conditions at the feet of her
emaciated enemy, which, in the vigour and
fullnefs of his health, fhe would not have accepted even upon her death-bed? that fhe is

fo

fo infenfible to the attractions of victory, if fhe were unmindful of every thing elfe, as to fub-mit to an infolent law of the enemy, which, in defeat and ruin, fhe would have refifted ? or that fhe will abandon her honour amidft the fhouts of triumph, which fhe would have defended amidft the cries of defperation ?—No, believe me, the government of France cannot fwallow this myfterious creed; they are not the dupes of this unreafonable and implicit faith, calculated only for the political methodifts of the day, for the illuminated commonwealth of Mary-le-bone fields.——Carnot and Lepeau are not amongft thefe true believers; they neither ex-pect the ceffion of Gibraltar, nor the circum-fcription of our marine, nor the repeal of the navigation act, nor the furrender of the Nether-lands, nor the dereliction of our allies, from *this* adminiftration, nor from *that*; all they re-quire or expect of their friends in England, is to difturb and embarrafs the government, and pro-tract the war; a fervice very faithfully rendered, and, I have no doubt, very honourably paid for; and to give appearances of diffenfion and ap-proaching revolt, fufficient to enable them to dupe and deceive their own people into a perfeverance, under this hope, which, without it, would be impracticable or defperate.

The government of France too muft have

taken into confideration, in any eftimate they
were forming upon the probability of affiftance
from the focieties, in cafe of invafion, that material point which I have already difcuffed, the
abfolute difgrace and extinction of the revolutionary principles which might have rendered
fuch an expectation lefs unreafonable at the beginning of the year 1793; they muft know
that as thofe principles have been unfolded and
difcredited, the danger of commotions, and the
danger in commotions, have fubfided along
with them, and they muft be diffuaded by their
own friends in thofe bodies from fo hopelefs
and fatal an experiment.

Though the defires, the ambition, and even
the embarraffments of the new government,
feem to prefcribe perfeverance on the part of
France, it does not therefore appear that they
can long find the means of perfeverance at
home, or that they can ferioufly rely upon any
affiftance, or upon any event very favourable to
their interefts in this country. This obftacle
to peace therefore being nothing more than the
perfonal obftinacy of the individuals in power,
muft yield to the current of events, and the
neceffity of the empire.

So well convinced does that government appear of the compulfion that awaits it, and of the
neceffity not only of renouncing the conquefts,

but

but of paying an indemnity to the powers at war, if it were to come to a negotiation, that it artfully throws all the conditions of peace into preliminaries, and exacts a previous assent, which would take away all occasion of discussion. This policy, however, at best weak and short-sighted, was desperate even at the time when their armies were triumphant in Germany; experience has doubtless undeceived the cabinet of France, if it ever really imagined that Europe would be frightened out of its liberties, and the Rhine be taken as it had taken Condé and Valenciennes, *by a decree of the Convention:* it must know, that this decree, as long as it exists, can have no effect, operation, or influence upon the conditions of peace, and maintain it only to render peace impossible, which, either from personal danger, or political fears, it considers it as a misfortune to itself, or to France.

The decrees, therefore, are not so much an obstacle to peace, as to negotiation, because, being wholly unfounded and unauthorised by the power, situation, and resources of France, they must necessarily fall at once, and without discussion, whenever that government wishes to have peace. Another obstacle to peace is, the indemnity of Great Britain, which will be less palatable to France, than the surrender of her precarious authority in the low countries. It is fortunate for her,

her, that she has a pledge in the magnanimity of this country, and in the personal character of the government, that it will not delay the repose and tranquillity of Europe, by exacting a rigorous justice, and retaliating upon her avarice and ambition. It is fortunate for France, that the moderation of her enemies will not pervert the successes of this war, to the attainment of any other objects than those for which it was undertaken, or direct the superiority of their arms, to any other end, than the vindication of the treaties, and the restoration of the balance of power.

Were it otherwise—but I repress myself; let her tremble to think, after the calamities of her military marine, after the extinction of her commerce, after the ruin of her finance, after the depopulation of her empire; let her tremble to think, what her case would be, if, with four hundred ships of war, with a commerce encreased, with an exuberance of resources, with a population untouched, and a constitution invigorated and endeared, Great Britain, in her turn, should remove the barriers, or violate the system of Europe; if, at the conferences for a peace, it were to be discussed, whether, after having been, during more than a century in danger of being enslaved by the natural preponderance of France, and, during the last years of being corrupted and annihilated

nihilated in all its political relations, by the arts and malevolence of that reftlefs country, by the overflow of its inhabitants, the univerfality of its language, and by a French faction in every ftate, I fay, whether it were not juft, expedient, and neceffary to the future welfare and tranquillity of this part of the globe, to provide for its fecurity, by circumfcribing her territory, and reftoring the ancient boundaries of her empire? Let her tremble to think, if fhe were to render all the ufurpations of the laft century, which juftice might-prefcribe, and her weaknefs fuffer, what limits would be thofe of France? how different from the Alps, the Pyrenees, the Rhine, and the Meufe?—I reprefs myfelf.—But France herfelf, if ever that country can be grateful, will one day own the obligation as all Europe befides does now. It is indeed glorious, after having ftood in the breach for civilized fociety; having repreffed the torrent of enlightened barbarifm, which threatened to overwhelm our arts, inftitutions, manners, and religion, and preferved the focial order upon its ancient bafis—to reftore the dyke, and rebuild the column: and with every thing in our power, to demand no more than the poft of honour, and the means of rendering the fame fervice, upon the recurrence of the fame neceffity.

This, I am perfuaded, will be evident in the terms of peace, which I have no fcruple to fay

muft

muſt and will be dictated by Great Britain. She will not abandon her allies for individual advantage, nor accept an equivalent for the uſurpations of her enemies; and the decline of the colonies with the ſeeds of a negro empire in the Weſt-Indies, will, in ſpite of the conqueſts ſhe may retain, render her a loſer in that part of the world. She will ſeek her true and certain indemnity, not in the arbitrary conditions, but in the firmneſs and ſecurity of an honourable peace; and this *Power of the third order*, will not forget, at a moment when every thing ſeems attainable to her ambition, that ſhe is the miſtreſs-nation, not by the extent of her territory and reſources, by a predominance of population, or a *natural ſuperiority over all Europe together*, but by her public and private virtues; her juſtice and moderation; her arts and induſtry; her laws and regulated liberty; her temperate courage; her unaſſuming wiſdom, and that moral greatneſs which ſhe oppoſes to every danger, and to the ſeductions of victory itſelf.

THE END.

---

Erratum page 1, lines 10 and 11—*to* this ſyſtem.

*This Day is Published,* Price 2s.

THOUGHTS on the ENGLISH GO-
VERNMENT, addreffed to the QUIET
GOOD SENSE of the PEOPLE of ENGLAND.
A Pamphlet attributed to Mr. REEVES, and
*ordered to be profecuted* by the HOUSE of
COMMONS.

———ALSO———

*Speedily will be Publifhed,*

An EXAMINATION of the above Pamphlet.
By JOSEPH MOSER.

www.ingramcontent.com/pod-product-compliance
Lightning Source LLC
Chambersburg PA
CBHW032355280326
41935CB00008B/582